ALASKA
FLYING

Surviving Incidents & Accidents

JAKE JACOBSON

Alaska's Favorite Real Life Wilderness Storyteller

PO Box 221974 Anchorage, Alaska 99522-1974
books@publicationconsultants.com—www.publicationconsultants.com

ISBN 978-1-59433-614-0
eBook ISBN Number: 978-1-59433-615-7
Library of Congress Catalog Card Number: 2016932009

J.P. "Jake" Jacobson
Alaska Master Guide #54
PO Box 1313
Kodiak, Alaska 99615
website: www.huntfish.us/
email: huntfish@ak.net

Manufactured in the United States of America.

Other books by Jake Jacobson are:

Alaska Hunting: Earthworms to Elephants, and *Alaska Tales: Laughs and Surprises.*

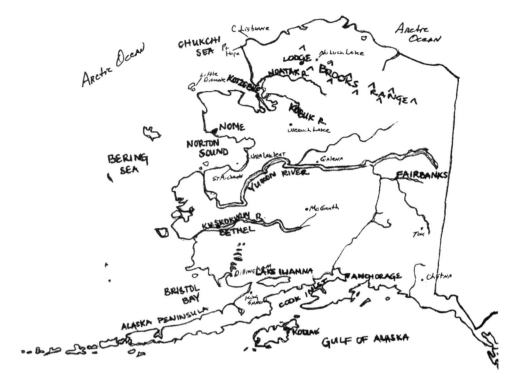

Map credit: Kate Jacobson

Contents

Testimonials

Alaska Hunting: Earthworms to Elephants

A rare gem about life and hunting in Alaska, by Utah State Aggie

Henry David Thoreau wrote, "most men lead lives of quiet desperation, and go to the grave with the song still in them." Sometimes, a man leads an interesting life. Infrequently, one leads a consequential life. Rarely the two come together. If the rest of us are very lucky, that man is also a gifted natural storyteller. Over the course of a lifetime, Jake Jacobson, dentist, outfitter and guide, entrepreneur, and family man, has polished his stories like the jade and petrified mammoth ivory he has lifted from the Alaska outback. He has entertained generations of hunting clients in the cluttered comfort of his arctic lodge. Now, those stories can reach a wider audience in this volume. All that is missing is the smell of caribou stew and trail creek berry bread wafting in from the kitchen.

Jake Jacobson has produced a beautiful gem of a book. It is a collection of vignettes that are alternatingly moving, perplexing, heartwarming, and hysterical. A grandson experiences the magic of a first hunting trip. A famous hunting author is the butt of an elaborate practical joke. A former senator is chased from camp at rifle point. The writing style is conversational and engaging. A wealth of black and white photographs illustrate the stories.

I'm tempted to compare Jake to Peter Capstick Hathaway, Robert Ruark, or Patrick F. McManus, but that would be unfair. He's James P. "Jake" Jacobson, DMD, Alaska Master Guide #54. He is one of a kind, and this book guarantees that he will not go to the grave with the song still in him!

Alaska Hunting: Earthworms to Elephants
Great read & educational, by David A Johnson

Jake provides 46 years of natural history observations and perspectives on arctic and interior Alaska, Kodiak Island, marine habitats, plus fun perspectives on hunting, Alaskan characters and the Eskimo culture. Jake demonstrates a consistent ability to critically asses or analyze wildlife and fish populations over time and the environmental effects weighing upon these wildlife populations, from Kodiak Island to the most northerly portion of the USA, Barrow, Alaska.

Jake's book was entertaining while providing an educational activity, whether the reader, be the general public, naturalists, sporting folks, professional biologist, anthropologist, or geologist.

Jake actively maintained a journal, recording past and present activities, recording his interesting life with its predicaments, in daily jot downs, now luckily, these interesting life glimpses are available to us regular folks, in book form. This daily journal activity, by itself, is a lesson for all aspiring writers, to instill, as a habit, into their daily activities.

Alaska Hunting: Earthworms to Elephants
By an Australian reader, Robert J. Penfold

Having hunted and fished over much of Alaska over the past 35 years I have learned to love the place. Jake's book is inspiring as it describes the real Alaska, the rural lifestyle, the real people and the visitors who come to experience this great land and its significant challenges. Jake's impeccable records of instances provide great insight into the real world of the professional big game hunting guide life. His attention to detail and his affinity with nature old and new, with his collecting artifacts and jade and collecting a wide range of friends along the way add to his 40 odd years of experiencing what Alaska has to offer. As a professional hunter, his approach to good game management and good conservation and high ethics are a standout in this book. It is a great read that I could not put down once I began turning the pages. Congratulations on producing a great book, the first of many I hope.

Alaska Hunting: Earthworms to Elephants
By C&N Geoffroin

As a long time resident, I love Alaska and all the adventure that it offers. I also enjoy reading about the adventures of others. As a result, I have several hundred books related to hunting, trapping and flying in Alaska.

Jake's collection of stories is as good as it gets. He writes in a descriptive and down to earth manner. Unless you have experienced it, it is hard to grasp the intoxicating nature of hunting and flying in Alaska's remote backcountry. Jake does an excellent job of taking you along for the ride.

Additionally, his stories illustrate the depth and knowledge he has gained in more than 45 years of guiding in Alaska. Each chapter and story holds your interest and you find yourself wanting to read on to the next. It is obvious that the author is an accomplished outdoorsman and knowledgeable about the species he pursues.

In conclusion, I give this book a five star rating—you will enjoy it. I suspect the author has lots more stories . I hope so, as I am looking forward to his next book.

Alaska Tales: Laughs and Surprises
By Ronico

A thoroughly enjoyable read! What a refreshing departure from the ho-hum of so much written material! This collection of short stories related to Alaska hunting details various aspects of modern Professional Hunting in our northernmost state. It focuses on dealing with the occasional absurdity of human nature, the vagaries and idiosyncrasies of people, including guests, guides and peripheral personnel. Jake dissects events, locating the humorous aspects of what might otherwise be completely negative scenarios. He sees the humor, sometimes adding to it, and makes the best of situations, however bizarre they might be. Legends and superstitions are explored and in some cases--exploited. If the reader is looking for relief from everyday "Great White Hunter" stories—give this publication a read. It will lighten your load and give you relief from the doldrums of average, everyday existence. My ribs hurt from laughing.

Alaska Tales: Laughs and Surprises

By Bulawayo

As thoroughly enjoyable as his first book. A great read.

Alaska Tales: Laughs and Surprises

By Utah State Aggie

I believe in full disclosure. I wrote one of the forewords for this book. I also believe in standing up and being counted for something you believe, like God, country, family, honor, and hard work. I wrote that foreword, and I am writing this review, because I believe that Jake has produced another wonderful little book that is worth every penny of your hard earned money. And in case you're wondering, no, I have no financial interest in Jake's literary efforts.

Jake's first book, *Alaska Hunting: Earthworms to Elephants*, is mostly about hunting. This book is mostly about people. Alexander Pope said, "The proper study of mankind is man." Too many of us shuffle through a grey world, staring with tunnel vision at our own feet. Jake has spent his wonderful, bohemian life training his clear hunting guide's eye not just at caribou and Dall sheep, but at all of us. He captures people in all our infuriating glory, and with all our contradictions, nobility and fallen nature. It doesn't take many of these stories to realize that Jake loves people. No one sees, and writes with this kind of detail without loving the subject. And yet he takes us on our own terms, painting a sympathetic portrait of each quirky character, hero and coward, saint and sinner. Because in the end, it is hard to tell which is which.

This book is definitely worth the money and is worth the time to read it. Actually, it is worth the time to read it five or ten times, or maybe more. Because, trust me, you won't just read it once.

Alaska Tales: Laughs and Surprises
By Craig Boddington

I have been fortunate to spend time in the Alaska wilderness with Jake Jacobson...aside from being a very genuine Alaskan legend--not just as an outdoorsman, but one of the early "flying dentists" serving Arctic communities--he's a real character and truly a funny guy. Read the "laughs and surprises" of his Alaska Tales, and you'll feel like you're seeing his wild Alaska...and laughing along with him.

Alaska Tales: Laughs and Surprises
By David A Johnson

The local chronicler, story-teller or relater of tales! A mostly lost or forgotten art form. As young whipper-snapper I much longed for the visit of the local story-teller. Mother, told me not to repeat the words 'story-teller' for it connoted the concept that the tales could be fictitious. Looking back fondly on my childhood days in the 1940s, entertainment was, for the most part, derived from vocalizations, either over radio-waves or person-to-person. Those tales or local stories were the glue that held our communities (family, town, district, state and country) together. The chronicler entertained, educated, and pointed out those little bits of shared human interactions which formed important relationships, especially in Jake's isolated and rural communities in Alaska. Most readers, because of circumstances, will never be able to visit or live in Jake's wonderful, yet challenging, area of northwest Alaska (plus other remote locals), yet readers will enjoy a chance to vicariously share a taste of Jake's wilderness adventures over his past 50+ years.

Alaska Tales: Laughs and Surprises

By Martha A. Stewart

Jake Jacobson does it again with a delightful read of unique Alaska adventures. Looking forward to his third collection.

Introduction

As soon as I arrived in Alaska I could see that flying was the key to making the best use of my free time, which I planned to spend enjoying the vast, beautiful wilderness—while out in it! But the cost of acquiring and maintaining an airplane was daunting. And, I wasn't making much money, plus I didn't have any flying experience, other than a few flights on commercial airlines.

In the course of performing my duties for the United States Public Health Service, I had to depend on large commercial airlines to get from one major town to the next. Then, once in a bush hub community, I usually needed to fly to the smaller villages by getting on a mail plane or chartering an air taxi.

On a trip to Lake Iliamna I met Lonnie Alsworth, who had a small airplane of his own and flew for a local air taxi. We became immediate friends and within six months of my arrival in the Great Land, Lonnie told me of a used Stinson Voyager airplane in flying condition which was for sale in Kenai for one thousand dollars.

Compared with the sleek Piper Super Cubs, the Stinson looked a bit overweight and stodgy, and had only an seventy-five horsepower engine.

But Lonnie said it would work for wolf hunting until we could afford a Super Cub. I became sixty percent owner in the Stinson. Our wolf hunting efforts soon paid for the airplane.

Using the G.I. bill I acquired my Commercial, Instrument, Multi-engine, and sea plane ratings. I did not intend to fly commercially, but when a request came to fly and work for the Alaska Department of Fish and Game on wildlife projects, I eagerly accepted. So my commercial flying came in through the back door.

Why Did I Write These Stories?

For the past several years I have been spending my winters on Kodiak Island. The second hatch of two children are both off to the university in Fairbanks. We get a lot of lousy weather in Kodiak. I have more uncommitted time on my hands than ever before.

Often memories of previous events come sneaking back into my consciousness. Sometimes a deja vu situation triggers them, but most commonly they just float up to the top of my store of recollections. Most often these reflections are of humorous or happy events, whereas the negative ones seem to fade to obscurity. On occasion, I recall an event which was instructive, some of which I relate in this collection of short stories. It is my hope that possibly readers will avoid some of the problems I have encountered either personally or anecdotally in my nearly fifty years of flying in bush Alaska.

Statistically, half of all plane crashes are due to pilot error, which includes navigating through dangerous weather (scud running), inadequate response to mechanical issues or ineffective handling of the aircraft on take-off or landing.

Though most of the incidents and accidents involving small aircraft are attributable to pilot error, there are some exceptions such as in-flight engine failure, metal fatigue, and collisions with birds—to name a few.

Mistakes I've made have been due to inexperience, ignorance, carelessness, and yes—neglect, among other things, but whatever the cause may have been, all of my mistakes and some of those of others have been learning experiences for me—instructive pot holes in the road of life.

So I hope that these stories may lead others to avoid making some of the mistakes noted in this collection.

Early Flights as Pilot in Command—The Club

After cutting loose from the Iliamna Lake Lodge enterprise, I concentrated on making a living at dentistry and was enjoying it immensely, but I did not want to become a forty hour per week, town dentist. Throughout rural Alaska, dental providers were scarce and, as I'd been delivering dental care to bush communities for the past two years, I had the experience and mind set for itinerant dentistry and I was strongly attracted to the independence and travel about the great state that sort of practice would afford me.

During my first winter as a private dentist I worked on getting some flying ratings under the G.I. Bill at Merrill Field in Anchorage during the mornings, while working as an associate dentist for an older fellow with an established practice downtown from noon until I ran out of patients in the evening. Normally I closed the clinic after 10pm.

My close friend, Lonnie and his Dad, Babe Alsworth, had given me plenty of practical instruction and had soloed me in Babe's Piper Super Cruiser in 1968, but I had to take the written exam and jump through the other hoops for proper licensure. I soloed after a couple hours of instruction, passed the written without a problem and started working on my Commercial license.

It was not so unusual in those days for an Alaskan to learn to fly in the bush without certified flight instructors. Some actually went on and got licensed by the Federal Aviation Administration—I was one of those.

At the end of a field trip to Kotzebue in March,1970, with about fifty hours as pilot in command logged, I agreed to fly a fellow's Piper Colt (PA22) to Anchorage, but only if he made the trip with me. He'd bought the airplane, referred to by local bush pilots as "the super Club," with the intention of making a bundle of cash by flying bootleg booze from Nome to Kotzebue, which was "dry" at the time, while liquor could be purchased in Nome. According to rumor he had scared himself on his first flight with the airplane and now wanted to get rid of it.

The Colt had a 108 horsepower engine which should give it about a 94 knot cruise speed. It was a tricycle airplane which made it not at all good for off airport or short field work, but I was interested in making the trip, which would be my longest cross country flight to date. The "Cub" was on wheels, so we checked with FAA to be sure that runways in Galena and McGrath were plowed. I was confident that Merrill Field in Anchorage would be good for wheels. We'd need to buy fuel in Galena and McGrath and both stations reported fuel availability and runways suitable for wheels.

It was about minus twenty degrees the morning of the scheduled trip and the catalytic heater had not stayed hot inside the engine cowling. We borrowed a big Herman Nelson heater and got the engine and interior warmed up nicely. As the heat was flowing, I began a thorough inspection of the plane—at least to the limits of my very limited ability. First, I noticed that the brakes were low on fluid, so we added some. Next I found that the controls did not freely go to maximum position, and discovered a bent aileron, so we warmed that up and tweaked it by bending it by hand into full functioning mode. There were several small cracks in the Plexiglas windows, so I borrowed a drill and stop-drilled them. It would be bad news for even a side window to crack all the way and break out during flight, and that was more likely to happen in very cold conditions, such as those at hand. By the time these repairs were done, it was well past noon and I did not want to risk making my first flight through the Alaska Range after dark, nor did I relish the idea of overnighting in McGrath. The trip from Kotzebue to Anchorage is a long flight with a reduced margin for error in winter and I wanted as much going for me as possible. Much to the disapproval of the owner, I said that either we wait until morning, or he could go it alone. He groused that I, with so little experience should decide to delay the trip. I deferred mentioning that with his greater experience he should have taken care of the deficiencies long before we were set to make the trip. I stuck with my decision. He had no interest in going alone or even operating the plane by himself. If I'd been smart, I probably would have decided against making the trip at all, but I wanted the experience and the additional hours for my log book. Such desires can lead one into big trouble.

That night we plugged in borrowed electric heaters for both the engine and the interior and the next morning everything looked right. We kept our gear to a minimum, taking only a couple of tarps, sleeping bags, a shotgun, an ax, small shovel and a borrowed catalytic heater that we were assured worked, and a gallon of blazo fuel. We took two thermos bottles full of coffee, some sandwiches and some candy bars.

Our departure was uneventful, but I soon learned that the cruise speed was going to be only about 85 knots and that the cabin heater was inadequate, but workable if we held the flexible hose close to the front windshield to keep it defrosted. We had only some hand held Sectional Charts and a compass for navigation, so pilotage was going to be critical. That's the main reason I insisted on the owner coming along. As it turned out, the need to have someone to frequently scrape the frost off the windows was crucial. He'd never made the trip before either, but he would be useful in keeping the charts handy and helping to keep track of the terrane features below us as we passed. Any country looks a lot

Not the "Club," but a Piper Tri-Pacer—in much better condition than the 108 horsepower Colt I was flying.

Piper PA-22 108 Colt

Performance and Specifications

Horsepower: 108
Gross Weight: 1650 lbs
Top Speed: 104 kts
Empty Weight: 940 lbs
Cruise Speed: 94 kts
Fuel Capacity: 36.00 gal
Stall Speed (dirty): 47 kts
Range: 415 nm

Takeoff and Landing

Ground Roll: 950 ft
Ground Roll 500 ft
Over 50 ft obstacle: 1500 ft
Over 50 ft obstacle: 1250 ft
Rate Of Climb: 610 fpm
Ceiling: 12000 ft

different with full winter snow cover than during summer, but, as a means of comforting myself, I reasoned that the paper charts look the same no matter the time of year or weather.

We flew over Buckland village after about an hour and kept flying on toward Galena. Snow cover was heavy on the ground, but we identified Wrench Lake and kept on, crossing the frozen Kateel and Gisasa Rivers, then the Koyukuk River before landing at Galena, where we topped off the fuel tanks. After relieving our bladders and jumping around to work out the kinks and warm up, we jumped back in and I steered for McGrath. We picked up a little tail wind, which was most welcome, as the temperature had dropped to minus twenty-eight degrees on the ground and was showing minus thirty-five degrees outside air temperatures at our altitude of 3,000 feet. My feet were cold even though I was wearing "bunny boots" and kept moving my toes.

We ran into snow squalls over the Yuki River but managed to hold pretty much on course. The runway at McGrath had been freshly plowed, but braking was minimal which necessitated a couple of blasts of throttle power to keep us straight after touching down.

Neither of us passed up the chance to jump around and stomp our feet in our efforts to warm up a bit as soon as we deplaned. Again we topped off the fuel cells to thirty-six gallons total, and wasted little time getting our bladders drained, our stiff spots exercised, and some of the kinks in our anatomy worked out. We were soon again airborne and en route to Rainy Pass. The pass was obscured in clouds and snow showers, so we took the longer route through Ptarmigan Pass. Before we reached Puntilla Lake the turbulence became uncomfortable, but we continued on, as there was no reasonable alternative. It was plumb dark when we crossed Knik Arm and set up to land at Merrill Field.

Wind was blowing 22mph and gusting to 35 coming from about 20 degrees to the left of the runway. I was tense and my passenger much more so, but I got it down and taxied to Polar Airways where I'd arranged with my mechanic friend, Voight Clum, to temporarily tie the Club.

It was a good trip, I'd learned several things and had to use some techniques as I had been instructed to do, but in conditions I had not hitherto encountered, but most of all, I was glad it was over.

My First Airplane

The winter of 1969–70 I made all my dental trips to rural Alaska by commercial airlines, except for the trips to White Horse and Dawson, in Canada's Yukon Territory, Tok and Valdez, for which I drove my truck. With the prospects of an oil pipeline to be built, Valdez was starting to boom, but as yet the town had no resident dentist, so I made several trips from Kotzebue to Anchorage by airliner, then drove in my 1964 Ford pick-up. I rented one of the cabins at the Valdez Village Motel to use as my office while working there.

I had a Canadian National Dental License and drove over to Whitehorse, then on the way back, I made dental service stops in Tok, Northway and Glenallen as none of these communities had a resident dentist. Unlike most of my later trips, I took a dental assistant with me on that extended road ramble.

On that trip I encountered the most prolonged period of deep cold in November, 1969 that I have ever seen. The thermometer dropped to minus forty-four degrees, then plunged to minus sixty-six for two days, making all travel uncomfortable. My truck's interior heater set on full power was not keeping the windshield free of ice, so my dental assistant had to keep scraping the inside of the windshield as I drove. She had some Alaska time under her belt and didn't mind the cold too much. Most important, she did not complain.

The FAA and Weather Bureau had offered me a place to set up my clinic and overnight lodging at no charge if I would visit some of their bush stations. This worked out well, but in Northway an ornery bush entrepreneur controlled most of the available enterprises from the electrical power plant to the school bus contracts, and he operated a small hotel and restaurant as well. On day one of our two day clinic he came by to pointedly remind me that he owned the hotel and restaurant and he expected us to use them. No salesman, he was not the least bit friendly. I told him that we were quite comfortable with the facilities provided by the FAA and would be staying where we were.

In front of several waiting patients, the guy exploded and told me that I was a no good S.O.B. and he was going to call his senator about this intrusion on his rights as a businessman. His swearing would have put most Singapore sailors to shame. I suggested that he go ahead and contact his Congressman or whomever he wished, but in the meantime to take his foul mouth and carcass out of my clinic. He let go a flood of epithets and cuss words before wheeling around and slamming the door. Patients waiting to be seen told me that he was a notorious "tail ender" and cautioned me to never come through Northway flying an airplane from Canada, as he was also the customs agent and after our confrontation, it was a sure bet that he would make life miserable for me. The locals went on to describe his throttle hold on the tiny community and told me they were glad that I had stood up to him. Obviously the entire community resented that officious oaf.

Two days later as my assistant and I were departing to drive on to Tok, that offensive fellow was up on a telephone pole doing something with the lines and started cussing me out at the top of his voice. I pulled the truck over, grabbed my short ax from behind the seat and walked to the pole, with him still cursing me. I did not reply as I began to chop down the pole. I'd taken only a half dozen swings before he was hollering that I was threatening his life. A couple more chips out of the pole, and he shut up and began to work his way down. I didn't like the thought of tangling with him wearing those climbing spikes. I laid the ax aside and invited him to come on down all the way, but he stayed about twelve feet up the pole. He was boiling mad, but kept his nasty mouth shut until I climbed back in my pick-up. I was laughing at the fellow. His last rants were heard only by the wires, I reckon. My assistant was beside herself in laughter. We never heard another word about this incident from the FAA, "his" senator or anyone else. And I never flew a plane from Canada through his customs station, either.

By June, 1970 I had my Commercial Pilot license and was primed to buy an airplane. I'd decided that a Cessna 170 would be ideal, but Babe Alsworth convinced me that the extra power of a Cessna 180 was well worth the greater cost. He said I should get all the power and braking capacity I could afford, then learn to use them properly. It was good advice.

That month I flew up to Kotzebue on Alaska Airlines and set up in a small, run-down, but serviceable house that I had purchased the previous fall. My intent was to headquarter in Kotzebue due to the laid back nature of the community and its proximity to outstanding hunting and fishing country. I could make improvements on the house as time permitted.

I'd been kicking tires, shaking wings, and examining log books for several months and had been repeatedly cautioned to avoid airplanes that had been owned or operated by air taxis, guides, or Natives. That was the common wisdom of the time. Guides and air taxi operators were known for selling their aircraft only after they had pretty well used them up. And a lot of Alaskans disparaged the way Natives maintained their equipment.

While checking a fellow's teeth in Kotzebue, he mentioned that he heard I was looking for an airplane and one was available. The owner was an air taxi operator, guide, and happened to be a Native Alaskan, who I had previously met, and he impressed me as being a fine man. His name was Tony Bernhardt. He lived up to his sterling reputation. Tony had purchased a Helio Courier and needed to sell his 1959 Cessna 180. That evening I went out to the field to see the plane. It was bare aluminum, except for some green and white trim and it had Federal hydraulic wheel skis—the best type. It had a little five channel VHF radio and an HF radio with a trail antenna. The HF would be good for long distance trips. There was no navigational radio, but one could be added if I purchased the plane. I liked the airship and the price was ten thousand, five hundred dollars, which seemed reasonable.

As I had but few hours as pilot in a plane with that much power or speed, I arranged for some instruction. A local school teacher friend named Bill asked if he could get checked out in the plane too, with the promise of accompanying me on my upcoming trip to Anchorage. That sounded like a fine deal. I wanted to get down to Dillingham, King Salmon, and Naknek while fishing was still in full swing and people had money to spend on dental care. The Indian Health Service did not make dentures, so there was a huge demand for prosthetics services.

Both Bill and I had some experience in tail draggers with up to 150 horsepower engines. This Cessna had a 230 hp engine with a variable pitch propeller and was a whole lot more machine to manage. Warren Thompson agreed to check us out in the Cessna and reminded us as he was instructing, "Ya gotta be thinking about a mile ahead with a one-eighty and if she starts to head for the bushes, hit the rudder pedal hard and be careful with the toe brakes. He cautioned me to always give it full aileron into the wind on cross wind landings and takeoffs and push the yoke full forward when taxiing down wind.

"Ya got lots of power with this airplane which will keep you safe if you learn to use it properly. Most of all remember, no animal is worth the airplane, so be cautious when choosing gravel bars to land on, especially if a big moose or caribou is what's calling you," he told me.

Two hours of instruction with Bill and I alternating at the controls had us feeling cautiously competent. We practiced landing on the paved strip, the dirt strip and some nearby gravel bars.

The evening before our planned trip to Anchorage, my friend Bill called to tell me that he just couldn't make the trip with me. Something had come up. I was disappointed, remembering how important the second guy was in keeping the maps handy on the trip I'd made the previous March, but I'd just have to go alone. I had only a compass and sectional charts for navigational aids. But, I planned to depart with much more daylight in June than we'd had in March, and I had a much faster aircraft. Besides, I had made the trip once before. The night before my departure I carefully plotted my course and drew the route in a bold line on my sectional charts.

It was rainy with towering cumulus clouds everywhere that day. I tried to navigate around the big thunderheads, keeping an eye on the chart and terrane, which looked far different than it had in winter. But I made it to Galena, where I topped off the fuel tanks and drained my bladder.

The next stop was McGrath, however the clouds were thicker and the air was more turbulent down that way. After going around a big cumulus cell I realized that the terrane did not conform to my supposed position on the map. It was hard to admit—even to myself—but I was lost!

After some poking around, looking for terrane that matched my chart, my fuel gauges indicated that I had less than an hour of flying time. I let out the High Frequency trail antenna and gave a call. Warren Thompson was on duty in Kotzebue and told me to keep talking, which I was happy to do. Then he told me to key the mike on a VHS frequency to get a DF steer. I did that and McGrath radio boomed in on my HF and said to steer 360 degrees. I told 'em I couldn't do that, as a huge mountain was right there. Next, they told me to steer 180 degrees. I had reservations about their advice and competency at that point, but I saw no obstructions to the south, so I turned to a 180 degree heading, and in about twenty minutes I thought I recognized stream meanderings below me that looked like the Nixon fork of the Kuskokwim River. From there, it was easy navigating on to McGrath where I was relieved to land and fuel up.

Before I found the Nixon Fork, when the possibility dawned on me that I might have to put the plane on a short river bar or another less than ideal place, I ate a candy bar and drank a can of Pepsi to get my blood sugar high. This was to hopefully avoid shock if my landing did not go well, and I got injured. Thank God it was not necessary!

This time, unlike the previous March, I lingered a bit in McGrath, visiting the Flight Service Station operators and thanking the men for their assistance. Then I started up, taxied out, and headed for Rainy Pass.

I made it to Anchorage just fine and the next day weather looked okay, so I flew south through Lake Clark Pass and on down to Bristol Bay, setting up my field clinic first in Dillingham, then King Salmon and finally Naknek. For years the Indian Health Service had provided very few dentures for people, so I got a lot of requests for "plates." The fish were running and money was flowing, so lots of folks wanted to get some "faults" teeth. I would take the impressions, then the "bite," have the patient help choose the teeth shade and shape from samples I showed them, and mail or air freight the models to a lab man in Anchorage. The lab man would expedite my cases and get them back to me within a few days.

In Naknek, I had a couple opportunities to further my friendship with Jay Hammond over dinner at his home.

The 1970 seasonal trip to "the Bay," as Alaskans call Bristol Bay, was financially good for me, so when I returned to Anchorage I spent a thousand dollars to have an Automatic Direction Finder (ADF) radio installed in the plane to avoid situations like the one I had encountered getting to McGrath. I decided to go "whole hog" and added a VHF/VOR radio as well for another six hundred bucks.

That Cessna was ideal for me. The rear seats consisted of a double sling seat which was hung on top and bottom pipes, easily removed to convert the entire rear, or only half of it, into open cargo space. The front passenger seat could also be easily removed to provide a place for extra heavy items, resulting in improved weight and balance with the center of gravity more forward, which improved overall performance.

The first fall, Mae and I made several hunting and fishing trips and had our freezer full of prime moose, caribou, salmon, sheefish and other wild meat before I began doing dental trips to Barrow, Valdez, Bristol Bay, Nome, Unalakleet and smaller villages. In all, over the next two years I visited fifty-seven different small towns or villages all over Alaska, except for the southeast panhandle area.

In each town I hired a local woman to serve as my dental assistant. Not only did I need the help, but I had an advocate to set things up prior to my arrival, to field questions in my absence, and be a full time witness to how I operated and treated patients.

Inevitably, some people will have complaints, but those few that were aimed at me were of minimal significance and none grew into destructive rumors, as my assistants were there to respond and they relayed patients' comments and concerns to me, to which I responded as soon as possible. I refused to ever restrain a child. Instead I would visit with each kid, preferably with a parent present. If a child was uncontrollable, I told the parents that their kid should be seen by a dentist that used sedatives. People were pleased to have dental services available to them and showed their appreciation in various ways. I got many invitations to dine with my patients, especially in the smaller communities.

A patient of mine from Nome wrote a short article about my bush dental practice, and the November, 1971 issue of the Alaska magazine ran it with two photographs of me and my airplane. The photo of me loading the plane amidst snow drifts was used on the front cover of "Bits and Pieces of Alaskan History, Volume Two 1960-1974.

On most long trips, I took my black labrador, Zeke, who loved to fly, but would hide his head in his paws in bad weather. Cafes in Valdez, Dillingham and most other small towns would welcome Zeke to the main dining area and provide him with a plate of scraps and sometimes special treats. My dog stayed in the clinic as I worked and provided an interesting diversion for patients, especially children. Zeke was my only traveling companion on those lengthy trips and I could not have had a better one.

I'd had some memorable "white knuckle" experiences with adverse weather and ground conditions on landing or taking off, but the power of that engine, the wheel/skis, the effective braking and sometimes my patience to wait for better conditions, pulled me through without accident or damage.

In late August, 1971, Mae and I had flown up the Noatak River to look for caribou. It was a windy, turbulent day. I looked at a short but adequate gravel bar that was shaped like an "I." The longer leg was directly cross wind, but the water adjacent to it appeared to be calm, showing no riffles from the wind. The other leg was uncomfortably short. I decided that the conditions favored the longer leg and set up to land. Once I had touched down and was committed to the landing with no opportunity to go around, I found that indeed, the cross wind was strong and it took all the aileron and breaking available to hold the plane on the bar and get stopped. What a surprise! I got out and walked to the water's edge to discover that it was completely frozen over with smooth glare ice that had made it appear to not be disturbed by the wind. That was a good, inexpensive lesson that I never forgot.

After a cup of coffee, Mae, Zeke and I got back in and I began to taxi to the end of the bar. One spot of soft sand required extra power and as I topped out on a small rise, one wheel hit a stump that I had not seen. The impact brought the tail up, causing me to hit my head on the "V" brace, but the tail came down without a prop strike. I'd lucked out again. I got out and carefully walked the area. It was another cheap lesson. Thenceforth I would always walk the strip, carefully looking for potential hazards. It's never good to be in too much of a hurry with an airplane.

As we flew on, I told Mae that I realized just then, that if I wrecked the plane, I would replace it with another. Prior to that, if I had a bad wreck, I'm not sure that I would have bought another airplane.

———◎———

In late April, 1972 I got some state "capitation" dental contracts for some villages in the Bristol Bay region. The hydraulic wheel skis were still on the plane and snow was heavy throughout Alaska. I flew from Kotzebue down to Dillingham, held a three day clinic there and went up to Pedro Bay on Lake Iliamna. New snow the night before I was to depart had not been cleared from the ice strip on Lake Iliamna, but I figured it would be okay. The snow was very sticky and when I got to the end of the short strip I pulled down full flaps, but the plane settled into the uncleared drifts. As the skis hit the snow drifts my visibility went to near zero, but I kept the flaps on with full throttle and after some spooky bounces amidst billows of snow, I was airborne. It was sure good to have all that horsepower! I was glad I had listened to Babe Alsworth.

After a couple days and nights in Igiugig, I departed one afternoon for my next and last stop, which was Levelock on the Kvichak River. It was showing signs of breaking up, so I looked over the landing strip. It was muddy with deep ruts showing. Even with wheel skis, I thought the danger of nosing up was too great, so I flew down to King Salmon and spent the night at the FAA facility. It was forecast to drop to plus twenty degrees that night, which I hoped would freeze the mud enough to permit a safe landing early the next morning. I was airborne just before sunup and when I arrived at Levelock the strip looked hard frozen. I set up for a soft field landing. As soon as the main wheels touched, the plane lugged down, the windshield was covered in mud and the tail started to come up.

I was blinded by the mud on the windshield and dared not attempt a go-around. I gave it a blast of power with yoke full back, which brought the tail down. Using brakes and rudder I was able to keep the plane going down the center of the strip. My roll out was significantly reduced by the mucky conditions.

A local fellow came along in a jeep and transported my gear to the school. We washed the plane off enough for me to see for take off and I

On wheel skis at Levelock airstrip.

landed with skis on the snowy edge of the Kvichak River which by then was flowing in the middle. I knew I had to get my work done quickly and get off that river or risk loosing the plane. The breakup was rapidly progressing and I was nervous about my departure.

The school population was small and everyone was very cooperative. I worked past midnight the first day and all day through until eleven the next night. On the third morning I was loaded and ready to squeeze the Cessna off the remaining bit of snow bank, but fog enveloped the area. I sat until noon, not knowing how much of a "runway" would be left. When the fog cleared, I walked what remained of usable snow. It was marginal, but I was low on fuel and therefore lighter than usual, so I fired the engine up and was blessed with a wobbly, but successful take off. I pulled full flaps at the end of my snow strip and was airborne with absolutely no runway to spare. After breaking ground, with the stall warning blaring, the plane was soft on the controls, so I lowered the nose as much as I dared to gain airspeed and staggered down stream, just above the open water.

The flight to King Salmon was short and uneventful, but when I landed, Flight Service people told me that they had an emergency dental situation due in from a cannery, so I set up again and wound up staying three days before weather allowed me to fly back to Kotzebue.

My airplane's main use was for transporting me and my dental gear to remote towns and villages, but I enjoyed using it for hunting and fishing as well—every chance I got.

Each year, beginning in late February, polar bear guides began to show up in Kotzebue, Nome, Teller, Shishmaref, Point Hope, Barrow and Barter Island. These villages were the most popular polar bear hunting bases and Kotzebue was known as "the polar bear hunting capitol of the world." Pairs of Super Cubs would fly out from their base village with a guide/pilot and one hunting guest in each aircraft.

There were a few exceptions to Super Cubs. At least one guide operating out of Kotzebue used a PA-12 (Piper Super Cruiser). One dentist/guide who, like me, was from the University of Oregon Dental School, used a Cessna 180 for his guided polar bear hunts out of Shishmaref.

Many of the cubs had extra fuel tanks installed inside their wings, outboard from the standard factory tanks, while others just carried as many five gallon cans of gas as they could fit in behind the passenger. Four and a half hours is normally all a fully fueled standard Cub will fly, but burning approximately eight gallons per hour, an extra twenty gallons or so allows a longer trip. It was common practice to carry a universal gear which could be used on either right or left side, in case a gear collapsed while on the ice. A spare gear could make the difference between loosing the aircraft or not, to say nothing of the lives and comforts of the people involved.

Commonly, each pair of aircraft returned to their base with the skins of two polar bears (*Ursus maritimus*) each day.

In March of 1971 I figured that polar bear hunting would soon be stopped, as there was so much clammer about it on the news. If I was ever to take an ice bear, it would have to be soon. My Cessna 180 was not ideal for the pursuit and I was inexperienced, but I figured I could make it work. I got lined up with a local fellow who had a Cub and we decided that we would hunt together until we each had a bear.

The forecast for the first day we had to hunt, indicated storm force winds to the north, but more reasonable conditions south, so we flew to Cape Prince of Wales, then across Bering Strait toward the Diomede Islands,

1971 Hunting polar bears off Wrangel Island.
A typical ice pan, bordered by pressure ridges.

giving Big Diomede and it's Russian garrison a wide berth. We turned northwest toward Cape Uelen on the Siberian coast, attempting to keep at least twenty miles from the shore, because the Soviets were know to be unfriendly toward hunters that got too close to their territory. As this was long before GPS, we were sometimes unsure of just how far offshore we happened to be. We just "eyeballed" it. Navigation "by guess and by gosh" was common back then.

The method we used was for the Cub to fly low, usually at about three hundred feet above the ice, with me following at six hundred to a thousand feet elevation, or so. To keep from overflying the Cub, I needed to keep one or two notches of flaps down, fly with the nose up a bit and throttle back to 1800 rpm, rather than the 2300 which I used for normal cruise. This makes for a tiring day of mushy, "soft stick" flying.

We found some good leads—open stretches of water, surrounded by ice, which are frequented by seals, which in turn are hunted by polar bears. The Cub would slowly sashay back and forth, looking for bears or tracks, both of which show up very well on clear, sunlit days. Upon finding a single set of large tracks, the Cub pilot would add a notch of flaps, slow down and follow. I would add another notch of flaps to slow my Cessna, which in such a "dirty" state (meaning low, slow and with flaps down) was continuously on the verge of a stall, calling for frequent power adjustments. Its a very tiring way to fly, especially for prolonged periods of time, and we were out for the whole day, which ran from eight to twelve hours, or even longer.

At times we landed and poured our canned gas into the wing tanks using a funnel and chamois.

That day we flew over several sows with cubs, three single bears that did not appear to be big enough and two freshly skinned carcasses. Other hunters had beat us to those two.

Our next opportunity to hunt showed weather similar to the first day, so we headed south again, this time turning west just north of Shishmaref. I knew two dentists, (like me, they were graduates of the University of Oregon Dental School) from Anchorage who guided bear hunts out of that village and they told me that a large lead on a 290 degree heading from Shishmaref had been producing good boar bears for them. They were done with hunters and going home, so they were happy to provide that information. We easily found the lead and it showed plenty of bear sign, but most of it was made by sows with cubs. We found no single bears that day.

A snowstorm kept us grounded for the next week, but a clear day with little wind followed and this time we headed northwest toward Wrangell Island. I had twenty cans of gas behind the front seats and the Cub carried four cans. I was carrying a total of one hundred and twenty gallons of extra fuel, which at six pounds per gallon, weighed seven hundred and twenty pounds. We would have to choose our initial landings with the extra weight in mind.

We departed Kotzebue in the dark, about five o'clock that morning, planning for a long day on the ice. We headed toward Point Hope, turning a bit to the west at Cape Thompson.

Out on the ice, most of the clear pans are absolutely flat with variable amounts of snow cover, bordered by piles of very rough, broken ice called pressure ridges, as can be seen in the photos. When on an ice pan, all one can see is the small area of the landing site and the jagged piles of ice on all sides.

Once a suitable bear was located, one airplane would urge the animal

Most polar bear show little fear of man and shots were at close range.

toward the pan where the other plane had landed. This "urging" was done by turning slow circles in the area opposite from the desired route of the bear. Polar bears are the most intelligent of all bears and they responded very well to this technique. The hunter on the ice would take a position amidst the broken ice of a pressure ridge and upon word from the guide at his side, he would shoot the bear.

When I heard of how these hunts were conducted, I was offended by the unsportsmanlike method. However, when one is in the hostile, danger-ous environment in which it takes place, it does not seem so reprehensible. The bear population was stable and could afford the loss of even more bears than were being harvested, so biologically, there was no reason to end the hunt. Still, I had some misgivings about the whole thing. But, in spite of all that, I wanted to see and experience it.

We kept flying northwest, searching every lead we found. One large area of open water was several miles wide, so we climbed higher and I kept especially tuned in to my engine noises. With a sigh of relief, we made the other side of the open water, descended, and went back to hunting.

Our second landing to refuel was close enough to Wrangle Island—several hours flight northwest of Point Hope—for us to see the shoreline cliffs. By then it was past midday and we decided it was time to turn back toward home.

Not wanting to retrace the route we had just traveled, we steered to put us a few miles further west, but still on a southeast heading. I spotted an aircraft on a pan of ice ahead and called my partner in the Cub. When we flew over it, we realized that the aircraft belonged to a guide we both knew who had told people in Kotzebue that he had lost his plane when a lead opened up on the pan he had landed on, and quickly swallowed his aircraft. It looked to us like the Super Cub had just been abandoned, but it was probably striped of radios and other parts, as indicated by human tracks around the plane. We figured the Cub was probably insured, as well.

Though not yet required by law, I had an Emergency Locator Transmitter and wanted to land, check out the Cub and leave the ELT at the deserted plane, then return with needed parts, including a new engine, to salvage that Cub. My partner in the other Cub wanted nothing to do with that enterprise, fearing potentially deadly reprisals from the guide who had probably made a claim on his insurance for the loss. I felt like I missed a great opportunity. Maybe I did.

We were feeling like we'd been snake bitten, as far as getting polar bears was concerned, when up ahead I saw several bears coming out of a hole on the edge of an ice pan good enough for landing. I got on my radio and told the Cub driver that I saw bears coming out of a hole in the ice, to which he said "Jake, that's not a hole, it's a wishing well!"

In all, I counted ten bears close to a heavily stained area near a pressure ridge. The area was colored by bear scat. The bears were a dirty yellow with darker stains on their front legs and hind ends. Three of the bears looked huge—the largest I had seen. The Cub landed and I peeled off to gently urge the bears back to the pan. The three biggest bears came back quickly, probably to reclaim whatever it was they were eating. I saw one fall as the hunter from the Super Cub fired. Then the guys from the Cub were standing over their kill. I had expected them to jump back in the Cub and go round up a big bear for me. I landed and urged them to get back in their plane and bring me a bear, as two big boars were still close by.

The pilot cranked his engine and was off, while I set up on the pressure ridge not fifty yards from my Cessna. Four polar bears came my way, one of which showed blood on its right front quarter. It was not one of the

Finally, I got a boar polar bear, long shadows indicate it was late in the day.

largest bears, but apparently it had been wounded prior to the big one being dropped. There wasn't a lot of time to deliberate the matter. I decided to finish off the wounded bear. Although it was not one of the huge boars, I was satisfied, given the circumstances.

As we'd flown several hours and were now lighter by several hundred pounds of fuel, we hurriedly skinned the bears, leaving the close fleshing to be done in town. I also put in both hind quarters of my bear as local Eskimos relish the meat, and I didn't mind eating bear meat myself.

We departed that pan just before dark and when the Automatic Direction Finder (ADF) acquired the Non Directional beacon (NDB) on frequency 356, we headed directly for Kotzebue. We had a long way to go after dark, but if we had nothing to run into until we reached the shore line, so no worries plagued us.

As we were well past the International Date Line, we flew from tomorrow, back into yesterday.

The large open lead seemed much wider when we flew over it in the dark, but I felt less concern, probably due to the high I experienced at getting a polar bear. We landed in Kotzebue just after one o'clock in the morning.

When the Marine Mammals Act was passed about a year later, hunting of polar bears was forbidden to all but coastal dwelling Alaskan Natives.

In the spring of 1973 some federal agents of the U.S. Fish & Wildlife Service stopped by my home in Kotzebue and told me that they were appalled to find the hides of sows and cubs stretched out in many of the villages.

Sows accompanied by cubs, of all bear species, were protected until 1974, when the bag limit for polar bears was raised from one bear every three years to three bears per day, including sows with cubs.

What the federal agents had not considered is the fact that Alaska Natives primarily hunt for meat, as opportunities present. Close to the Alaska coast, most of the polar bears are sows and cubs. The guides were taking most of their big boars much further out, normally in international waters or just off the Siberian coast.

So, prior to 1973, most polar bears were harvested offshore on international waters and the State of Alaska set the annual harvest limit at 300 bears per year. Beginning in 1973 all polar bears were taken close to Alaskan shores and no annual limit was set.

Wrench Lake—
an Unintended Stop

In late November, 1970 I was in Anchorage with the Cessna 180 after a dental field trip to Bristol Bay and Valdez. It was time to go home to Kotzebue for a spell. I'd owned the Cessna for nearly six months.

The day before my intended departure to the Arctic I happened to run into a neighbor who asked if I had room to take him along. He said he didn't have much gear to take. He wasn't a big guy, maybe weighing a hundred and sixty pounds in winter clothes and boots, so I said "sure, I'll take you." I would welcome the company on the long trip. There would be no cost to him, as I had to make the trip anyway. He seemed to like that news.

But days were short and getting shorter by about ten minutes per day, so I intended to depart my tie downs at Polar Airways on Merril field not later than six-thirty the next morning. That would put me on the south side of Rainey Pass as sunlight arrived and hopefully, with brief stops to refuel in McGrath and then Galena, I could land in Kotzebue before full darkness had arrived. Weather was forecast to be good VFR for the entire trip, but a large storm was coming and expected to hit the Kotzebue area sometime the day after. That storm was a big one, bringing with it a lot of new snow, so if I didn't make the trip the next day, I would likely be weathered out for two or three days. And I wanted to be home.

I reminded the fellow to be at Polar Airways at six o'clock the next morning and ready to go. He assured me that he would be there.

Most stores closed at nine in the evening and it took me until then to locate the last of the things on my list for transport to Kotzebue. I stopped by LaMex for a quick enchilada, fired up my catalytic heater at Polar Airways and put it inside the cowling, then did a pre-flight inspection on the aircraft. I made one last stop at a grocery store to buy a loaf of bread, lunchmeat and cheese for the trip. I added a couple of apples and got three pounds of white grapes. It was nearly eleven when I crawled into bed.

My alarm woke me at five o'clock and I noticed stars overhead. That was a good sign of fair weather, but it was cold. I brewed a pot of coffee and filled my thermos. My 1964 Ford pick-up started, thanks to the electric circulating water engine heater and I was soon loading my goodies into the Cessna, but my passenger had not arrived. I decided to give him a few more minutes to show up. As I impatiently sipped a cup of coffee at the Polar Airways office, my tardy passenger called in. He sounded tired and boozy as he asked if I could drive to the east side of Anchorage to pick him up. A round trip such as that would delay me by at least another hour, and he sounded so hungover I was not keen on his company anyway, so I told him I simply had to go and wished him good luck, especially with the hangover he obviously was battling.

I removed and capped the catalytic heater, stored it safely aft of the passenger seat and started the engine. I was thoroughly disgusted with my no-show passenger as I taxied to the runway. I crossed the Knik Arm of Cook Inlet and headed for Rainy Pass. But the Pass was obscured in clouds, so I took the longer route through Ptarmigan Pass, found the South Fork of the Kuskokwim River, flew by "Little Egypt," then Farewell and landed at McGrath in minus twenty-six degrees, but calm wind.

The fuel attendant was efficient and I was soon airborne and headed north by northwest to Takotna, then Ophir, and on to Galena. One cold sandwich of lunchmeat and cheese between a slice of bread, along with a cup of coffee kept me comfortable. Conditions were decent at Galena and again, fueling was done quickly in minus twenty-eight degrees and I was off on my final leg to Kotzebue. I had gained some time which negated that lost by waiting for my erst-while passenger and things were looking great for getting home, having a hot meal, and tucking into my comfortable, warm bed.

But as we all experience in life, sometimes things do not turn out to be as expected.

I flew on Victor Airways route V498, crossed the Gisasa River, flew over the hills to the Honhosa River and crossed the Kateel River. Once I got over the next low range of mountains I would have it all downhill to Kotzebue, but I was getting bounced around by increasing turbulence. Then I noticed that the small valleys below me looked fuzzy. It was blowing snow—a ground blizzard created by high winds funneling down the narrow valleys. As I flew on, the formerly friendly skies had morphed into a sullen overcast, and I could no longer see the riparian vegetation in the rivers and creeks below. I didn't like what was quickly developing into a serious compromise in visibility, along with the increased buffeting from the violent air.

By that time in my flying career I had logged about one hundred and seventy hours, most of which was in that same Cessna 180. I felt relaxed and competent, but I had resolved to maintain my intrepidity index at a cautious level. It became evident that the big storm forecast to hit the following day was, unlike my wannabe passenger, early in its arrival.

In August I had purchased and installed a King ADF which was invaluable on all flights and a VHF/VOR which was also advantageous, but I was out of range of dependable VHF communications. I reeled out the trail antenna of my HF radio, but failed to make contact with anyone. Nevertheless I had the VHF turned on at the highest volume setting and I picked up some partial transmissions by pilots indicating that Nome weather had deteriorated to IFR conditions. Then, on my ADF, I caught part of a broadcast of similar adverse conditions in Kotzebue. I began to consider an unscheduled stop. There were no villages or other runways nearby.

A well named lake was on my direct route and when I came to the easily recognized Wrench Lake, I realized it was decision time. The lake was plenty long enough for me to land directly into the wind and the plane had Federal hydraulic wheel skis which should slide me over any snow berms that I failed to detect—if they weren't too big. From six hundred fee above I could see the surface was bare ice in some places, but it was wind rowed with snow in other areas. On approach to land, once I was about one hundred feet above the frozen lake, I could no longer see the surface due to the blowing snow. After flying several practice approaches, I decided to pump the wheels up and use the skis for landing. I did not worry about any open water, as the outside air temperature was hovering around zero degrees Fahrenheit and it had been cold for more than a month.

The thought of sitting out this intense storm on a remote lake was not inviting, but the thought of getting into much worse conditions was even less so. I resolved to land, so I reeled in my trail antenna.

I tried to line up my approach by using a small point of land on the lake shore, but I lost sight of it as I reduced altitude. The best I could do was estimate and hope.

My altimeter had been set in Galena, but I was flying into an area of lower pressure so the rule "If flying from hot to cold or high to low, watch out below" came to mind. My actual altitude was likely lower than indicated on my altimeter, but as I was landing on a surface of unknown altitude, I would just have to go by visual contact. However I lost visual at about one hundred feet above the lake. All this was not too purty good.

On my final approach I used the entire length of the lake and flew the plane on as if I was doing a glassy water landing. As I reduced power I was tense, braced for an abrupt impact with a large wind row, but instead I felt only a gentle bump on contacting the lake surface. The wind was strong enough to slow my ground speed on touch down to about twenty-five miles per hour. My skis had found a long patch of glare ice. I continued to reduce the throttle. The skis bumped over small snow drifts and rattled. After I was nearly stopped, the wind was rocking the plane, so I added power to take me to the upwind side of the lake. I taxied close to a small bluff and stopped. The plane was showing less wind effects here, so I decided to sit for awhile and think things over.

I left the engine running as I deliberated on what to do next. Clearly I would need to secure the aircraft first, then decide whether to stay in the cabin, which was jammed with freight, or make a snow shelter. Trying to set up my tent was out of the question in that fierce wind, which I estimated at forty miles per hour with occasional gusts to sixty.

Then a thought flashed before me. In my disgust at my irresponsible passenger I had failed to file a flight plan and did not think of it while in McGrath or Galena. That was the only time I have neglected to file a flight plan to this day ... decades later.

Well, nobody would be coming out to look for me when I was late arriving in Kotzebue and that was a bit of a plus. I didn't want anyone out spooling around in that wild weather. My family knew I was inbound and would call friends if I did not show up, but I was on my own.

Had I filed a proper flight plan, I would have given my route from Galena to Kotzebue on Victor 498, rather than a less direct route up the

Koyukuk River or such. Any search effort would begin by following that route and likely see me on Wrench Lake. Oh well.

With an hour or so before official sunset I wanted to do as much as possible before full dark was upon me. After putting the engine cover over the cowling, I chopped a hole about fourteen inches deep beneath the left wing tie down ring, then another hole about a foot away. With my knife I tunneled between the holes leaving an ice bridge about ten inches thick between the holes. This would serve as a secure tie down for the wing. I cut similar holes for the other wing and made a set of holes to secure the tail wheel. Three half inch nylon ropes kept the airplane steady.

Wearing a pair of foam insulated gloves, my hands got painfully cold, so I put on my big pair of fleece lined mittens, providing an instant delight. As I was putting them on, a gust nearly ripped away one of the mitts. I had to be constantly mindful of the wind which tugged at everything in its effort to blow it away.

With only about fifty feet between me and the bluff I figured I could make a cave in the snow drift and remain close enough to the airplane and be much more comfortable than I would be inside the aluminum machine. And I would be out of that infernal wind.

Using a short handled shovel, I began digging a small burrow into the snow drift. The snow was hard packed and easy to hollow out for a shelter. It was almost like a sculpting procedure. There was no caving as I kept cutting more snow from the hole. I kept my cave entrance small, then after digging about three feet into the snow, I dug laterally on both sides to create a sort of "T" providing just enough room for me to stretch out on my sleeping pad.

I returned to the plane to get my sleeping pad and bag, my rifle, pistol, food, emergency gear, and a couple of small tarps.

I laid out one tarp on my sleeping area, then placed my pad and thick down sleeping bag on top before rigging the second tarp over the entrance. Any heat I generated would mostly be retained inside. It was cold and dark inside my cave and I was hungry, but I was feeling pretty good about the whole situation.

Before I indulged my appetite I placed a spare flashlight in my shirt pocket to keep it warm. My second cup of coffee was luke warm, but delightful. Two more lunchmeat and cheese sandwiches had me feeling pretty good. The apples were frozen, but I ate one.

Then I remembered the white grapes. They were hard as marbles, but I ate a handful and was surprised at how nice they tasted. Since that night I have always made it a point to freeze white grapes before eating them.

Leaving everything but my bunny boots on, I crawled into my heavy down sleeping bag and must have slept, as the next time I was aware of anything, my Timex wrist watch showed two thirty in the morning. I was too warm. I extracted myself from my cozy feather nest and wormed my way to peer outside the tarp. Some drifts had formed outside my entrance tarp, but there seemed no risk of my access being completely buried by the forming drift.

Between periods of zero visibility in blowing snow, I could occasionally make out the form of the Cessna, still in place, and facing straight into the wind, so I removed my down parka, rolled it to serve as a pillow and squirmed back into the bag. I ate a Mars candy bar and soon I lapsed into sleep.

About six hours later I awoke and noticed that the roof and upper parts of the walls of my snow shelter were partially glazed over with ice. Apparently my breathing had caused that. I put on my parka, booted up, and went to the aircraft to check everything. All seemed fine, the ropes were tight, and the wind seemed to be less powerful, but visibility was still restricted. Snow had packed in under the skis and drifts about a foot high trailed off their back edges. The outside air temperature gage on the plane indicated a plus fifteen degrees, which was considerably warmer than the previous afternoon.

The last of my day old coffee had lost all traces of heat and turned to slush ice, but I swallowed it, along with another sandwich, the remaining apple, and some more frozen grapes. I chuckled at my accidental discovery of the delights of frozen white grapes. I used my single burner Coleman stove to melt a pan of water, then added instant coffee, fake cream and sugar for a shot of regular starting fluid for my body. Two more more pans of hot melt water filled my thermos for drinking water later.

I had a full gallon of Blazo fuel for using with the catalytic heater—enough for two nights burning, but I decided to hold off until evening to decide whether to put it inside the cowling or not. I would not use any of that fuel for my personal comfort. I kept another quart of fuel with the small stove. I had once slept in a small room with a catalytic heater and developed a tremendous headache from the fumes, so there was no temptation to heat up my living space with the little heater, and I didn't need heat anyway. If the temperature warmed up to plus twenty degrees outside, I could safely start the airplane engine without pre-heating. My dop kit thermometer indicated plus twenty degrees in the snow cave.

By mid-afternoon I was sure that I would not be able to travel before spending at least one more night in my new abode, but the wind definitely was beginning to tire.

With time on my hands I walked around my end of the lake for a half hour or so, then dug out a pocketbook novel from the airplane. Reading always makes time go by enjoyably and inside the snow cave was no different. I also retrieved a jar of blackberry jam and a carton of Sailor Boy pilot bread for nice snacking fodder. I had plenty of food in the plane, enough to last for weeks, but I doubted it would be necessary.

By four o'clock that afternoon the temperature had risen to plus twenty-two degrees and the wind seemed less fierce. I had high hopes of making it on to Kotzebue the next morning. Not wanting to miss the first opportunity to depart, I decided to fire up the catalytic heater and put it inside the cowling, expecting it to cool down that night.

With the Coleman I heated up two cans of chili by placing a can directly on the flame until it "bleeped," then removed it to cool a few minutes before opening. Heated this way, the contents are never burned, and opening after a short time away from the flame, the initial opening does not result in a spurt of super hot juices. But one must be mindful of the "bleep" or the can could explode. A pan of melted snow made water for hot chocolate. I figured I was living pretty high, considering the circumstances.

The heat from the stove had transformed my cave into a better insulated, ice lined room. I was chilly, but not uncomfortably cold.

But I wasn't sleepy either, so by alternating flashlights from illuminating my book to warming up in my shirt pocket, I was able to do some reading until, finally I felt my eyelids lagging and was able to doze off to sleep.

Again I woke up at two thirty. I bellied over to the flap, peeked outside and saw the plane was still sitting pretty and the wind had slacked. The overcast was thinner and I could see the plane clearly this time, so I went back into the sack and was soon asleep.

At seven I was fully awake. Pulling aside the tarp I saw some stars and was thinking that I had probably spent my last night in the cave.

With at least three hours before I would have the benefit of maximum daylight, I melted more snow for coffee and munched down some pilot bread and jam before stuffing my sleeping bag into its sack and rolling up the pad. And I treated myself to more of those tasty grapes.

With the weather turning so civilized, I was worried that some of my buddies might be out burning gas as they searched for me and I wanted to avoid my embarrassment and their unnecessary effort, if I could.

Once my overnight gear was stowed in the plane, I used the shovel to smooth out some drifts and then walked the lake well beyond what I would need for a take off runway. I stomped a piece of cardboard into one drift to use as a marker. I had decent visibility now—probably five miles or so—and if I lined up parallel to the few wind rowed drifts I should become airborne without any problem. The temperature had dropped to plus ten degrees, so I was glad I'd used the heater on the engine.

Ready to go, I checked the oil which was full enough and a bit thick, but it sluggishly oozed off the stick. I double checked to see that the magnetos were off before I turned the propeller through twelve strokes to give the cold battery a little easier time. I kicked both skis to make sure they weren't frozen down. Grabbing the left wing strut near its connection to the wing, I wobbled the plane up and down to see that it was free. The wings and control surfaces were free of frost and snow.

Three shots of the primer and the engine coughed and fired on the first try. I let it warm up for a full ten minutes until the cylinder head temperature showed over one hundred degrees and the oil temperature was up to sixty. With the cabin heat on full hot I was already feeling toasty.

A burst of the throttle and the plane moved a foot forward. Another burst with full left rudder and Five Zero Echo turned as I began the taxi to my cardboard marker. Once at my marker I went again through all the preflight CIGAR procedures—Controls, Instruments, Gas, Aircraft trim and Run up. I had no way of setting my altimeter. Then I reviewed the other mnemonic GUMP—Gas, Undercarriage, Manifold pressure and

N5150E tied down in Kotzebue.

Propeller. After all the good luck ... or blessings I had just received, I sure didn't want some dumb, neglectful omission to cause me grief. I was feeling good about the take off and the prospects for arriving in Kotzebue soon.

The Cessna acted like it was as happy to be departing the remote lake as I was. With a head wind of only about twelve miles per hour we lifted off in half the distance I had figured for the runway and I was over my snow cave at a hundred feet and in a left turn in mere seconds.

With a broken layer of clouds at about thirty-five hundred feet, I climbed to just over three thousand and began calling on my VHF. After a half dozen calls over ten minutes time, one of the Shellabarger Flying Service charter pilots near Selawik heard me and relayed my estimated time of arrival to the Kotzebue Flight Service Station.

When I landed on runway 8, the snow drifts were huge on the south runway where I usually parked, but the north ramp had been cleared, so I taxied over to Shellabarger's. One of the pilots I knew came out and directed me to one of their spare spots to use until the airport maintenance crew could clear my own. It was good to be home.

When I walked into the little shack that served as a windbreak and coffee dispensary, Leon greeted me and said that one of my buddies had called asking if anyone knew of my whereabouts. He suggested that I call the fellow to calm his nerves. As I made the call, Leon handed me a cup of fresh, hot coffee. It was wonderful.

I offered the boys at Shellabargers some frozen white grapes.

Alaskan Flying Follies: Tie the Tail

Alaska is, no doubt, the flyingest place in the world and no high time pilots that I know can truthfully state that they were never responsible for a flying foible.

When Babe Alsworth was giving me flight lessons, he, among others, advocated always tying the tail, as well as the wings. Most pilots neglect that simple chore, no matter how little extra time and effort it takes, and some paid a heavy price for their sloth.

Back in the late 1960s one fellow, whom I shall not name, at Iliamna (the area is often referred to as "Mother of the Winds"), had just set up his own air taxi service and bought a brand new Super Cub. In spite of the notoriously strong winds which are apt to come from any direction at any time in that area, he, like the majority of small aircraft pilots, did not deem it necessary to tie the tail of his flying machine.

One dark night the wind came up, blowing fifty miles per hour. In a big wind like that gusts can be double or triple the main velocity, due to local effects, or simply the vagaries of storms. Sometime after midnight, when most good folks were asleep, the wind switched direction and was coming from the tail end of his Cub. A strong gust lifted the tail and another big puff pushed it on over, putting the beautiful little plane on its back.

The new commercial operator was stricken with grief and remorse when he arrived at his no longer beautiful and now, seriously damaged aircraft the next morning.

A major rebuilding job had the air machine back in service after several months and thousands of dollars out of pocket. He proudly flew it back home and tied it again in the same place. Once again, he did not secure the tail. Once again, the Mother of the Winds gave birth to a gusty blow child, but this time our neophyte airman woke up and dutifully drove his pickup truck to rescue the plane. He had not put anything in place to tie the tail down, so he reckoned the truck bumper would suffice. With his brain still befuddled by his interrupted sleep, he backed the truck up close to the tail and attached a strong line between the bumper and the tail spring of the Cub.

Relieved and somewhat proud that he had prevented an embarrassingly expensive and preventable incident such as happened only a few months before, he climbed back into the truck and drove off—collapsing both wings and twisting the fuselage of his newly rebuilt aircraft.

I cannot imagine the look on his face when he realized what he had done in his semi somnolent state.

Lessons to be learned: ALWAYS put an adequate tie down for the tail in place, permanently. Then USE the tail tie down—every time. And THINK before you do anything around an airplane.

Untie the Tail

My good friend, Leon Shellabarger told me that some years before he had needed to move his Super Cub off the sea ice in front of Kotzebue, as overflow water was coming up over the surface. He got it flying and landed alongside the North/South runway. He placed a full gasoline drum under each wing and tied them down, then he hauled in a one hundred pound propane bottle, tied the tail to that, and went back to bed. The Cub sat there for a couple of weeks, during which time snow had drifted around the barrels and covered the propane bottle. One day he had personally dug out the barrels before being interrupted by a problem at the hanger. When he returned, he untied the wings, but forgot about the propane bottle, which was buried in the snow drift.

Leon planned to move the Cub back to the ice in front of his lodge. After an adequate warm up, Leon added power, but the Cub seemed stuck, so he rocked the stick and goosed the throttle, finally resulting in some forward motion of the plane. He figured the bottoms of the skis were frosted, which would explain the increased resistance to movement. A little ground travel and the frost would clear itself, or so he figured.

So Leon kept at it until he got the Cub to inch its way to the runway.

Then he got more speed and took off, but with greater difficulty than he had expected. With his trim turned full nose down, the Cub was still flying nose high. He made a turn and looked back to see the propane bottle following a few feet behind. RATS! (Leon probably said something worse, but the reader gets the idea.)

The overflow water that had prompted Leon to move his Cub off the ice had receded, and the sea ice in front of his house was good for landing again.

The day was sunny and relatively calm, which brought a large crowd of people to the post office which sat just in front of Leon's ice tie downs. Witnesses aplenty saw his faux pas. The ice had been blown clear of snow, making a very slick, flat place to land. He touched down and kept adding more power to avoid being overrun by the propane bottle which was skidding over the ice in pursuit of the airplane. The crowd was thoroughly entertained.

Leon got the Cub stopped in his usual place, climbed out, tied the wings and walked across the short stretch of ice to his home for a beer.

When asked about the bottle as he walked past some of the hangers-out at the post office, he said that he was trying to avoid having to manhandle the thing out of the snow drift and into his truck, so flying it over was an easier way to transport a hundred pound propane bottle from the runway to his home, anyway.

Leon Shellabarger was an excellent pilot and usually could be depended upon to get in the last word, especially with hecklers.

No Good Deed Goes Unpunished

One of the old timer local plots in Kotzebue seemed to encounter a lot of bad luck, which often visited him while he was trying to do something good for some other soul.

One fine summer day this fellow, whom I'll call Lex, had come to Kotzebue for groceries in his Super Cub on floats. He got his shopping done and heard that a lady from his home village was trying to contact him. He got to a single side-band radio and learned that she had a gasoline powered boat and a small flat bottom barge in Kotzebue, loaded with materials, some of which were perishable. She needed the loaded barge to be taken to her store in the village. Her usual boatman was incapacitated. It was on Lex's way and although it would take at least twelve hours or more to tow the barge up river, rather than to simply fly home in an hour, Lex agreed to help the damsel in distress.

But Lex would need his plane when he got home. The wind was calm and the water was glassy flat, so he put a line on the float cleats of his Super Cub and towed it behind the barge, which trailed the power boat.

It was a most unusual, irregular, maritime daisy chain.

Wind was flat calm when he, now the maritime pilot, started out from Kotzebue, but as he was crossing the large estuary, called Hotham Inlet, the wind tuned up and started to blow plenty from the east—off the bow of the boat. Turning that water borne train around was not an option. The best thing Lex could do was continue on, into the wind, expecting to find shelter once he got inside one of the river channels a few miles ahead.

But sometimes things align themselves to go wrong and this was one such time. The plane began to list toward the right and before Lex could do anything to relieve the situation, the Cub sank. Luckily the brackish water was only four feet deep, but the tow line had to be released or the Cub would have been destroyed by dragging it through the muck, snags and flotsam. At least it was sitting on the upwind side of the estuary. The larger waves on the lee side would have torn the little plane apart.

Lex dropped anchor and rode out the blow, which diminished after only a couple of hours.

Crewmen from a passing skiff assisted in raising the Cub, its floats were pumped out, the tow line was reattached and the journey was resumed.

This was an untimely accident and an expensive one, requiring some repair work on the floats and desalting engine and interior of the Cub, but Lex had it back in service in less than a week. The salt content of the estuary was not high, or his damage would have been much worse.

Good Intentions Can Lead to Grief

My well intentioned, hard luck friend, Lex, came in one cold winter day in his Super Cub, landed on the ice in front of town and taxied up on the snow bank in front of the general store, Hanson's Trading Company. The east wind was offshore and moderately strong, at about thirty miles per hour. It was a typical winter day, but the force of the wind was broken in the lee of the building. My friend decided that tying even one wing would not be necessary, as he wouldn't be long in the store.

Lex hustled into the store and quickly made his purchases.

In the meantime a local fellow came by and noticed the Cub rocking in the wind, so he tied the right wing to a partially frozen fifty-five gallon barrel of honey bucket (inside pooper) contents. It was the kind of thing a thoughtful person would do for anybody, especially a good friend, and Lex was a friend to everyone.

When Lex raced back with his purchases, he stuffed them in the back of the plane and hit the starter, never noticing that the upwind wing had been tied. The engine coughed, then roared to life. Daylight is limited in the winter at that latitude and there was a fair piece to travel into a stiff wind, so when Lex pushed in the throttle and gave it full rudder to the left, he felt resistance to moving. He assumed it was due to a ski getting pinched in a crack in the ice, so he goosed the throttle several times. The Cub struggled to overcome the drag and eventually began to gain some speed. Lex kept wondering what was causing such a poor performance, but he was gaining speed, so he kept full throttle. Maybe the skis had picked up some gnarly ice on the bottom, he figured.

When Lex finally got airborne, he immediately felt, then noticed, that his right wing was low. A quick visual revealed that the problem was following him a few feet behind the wing. What a bunch of crap! A brownish trail of recently added, and as yet unfrozen, contents streamed from the container.

Being a thoughtful fellow, Lex steered for the ice, rather than fly over town spreading the awful, offal contents. Lex began thinking of an appropriate spot to lighten his load—to relieve himself—so to speak, of his burden.

As he flew along, Lex reasoned that four hundred pound plus pile of partially frozen poop would have way more momentum once he landed on the slick ice than the aircraft would have. A problem might arise as he slowed down. The barrel of "honey" would not slow down as rapidly as the Cub. It would be simply awful to be slammed by such a huge accumulation of strangers' poop—especially if there were witnesses.

Lex had endured some trouble in his life, but never before had he been threatened so relentlessly or so dangerously by such a hard s--t situation.

Lex decided on several things.

One: Definitely a landing into the wind was required.

Two: A smooth surface that would not cause the barrel to dig in and perhaps cause the plane to ground loop was called for, and

Three: A relatively private place, with no one around to see this hazardous maneuver and potential anointment if his landing went awry was to be preferred.

He found such a spot just north of town, a bit west of Pipe Spit.

Only someone who happened to be coming in to town with a dog team or snow machine would be close enough to see the landing, and no one was in sight.

Reminiscent of a man running to the outhouse with a bad case of scours, Lex decided to get 'er done.

He made a flat approach, just high enough off the ice to avoid the barrel contacting the surface until he was ready. A gentle reduction in power was met by a slight jerk on the wing as the smelly drum touched down and belched out some of it's contents. Then Lex added power intermittently, as needed to keep the plane ahead of its pursuer, or should I say ... its sewer.

But in a small town like Kotzebue, especially in the entertainment deprived times of winter, nothing goes unnoticed and all juicy news is soon reported.

Lex debarked from the cockpit leaving the engine running in expectation of a rapid departure, and holding his nose, he cut the offending tie down rope. As he turned to walk back to the plane, several snow machines roared up. Some villagers were headed to Kotzebue from a nearby community and they had witnessed his battle to avoid a debacle. And they were in a humorous mood.

Lex pulled the mixture to shut down the engine and endure what comments might come.

In deference to considerations of propriety I will not repeat the comments that were made and later related to me. Suffice it to say that most commentators offered congratulations to Lex, amidst raucous guffaws and colorful what-if's.

It was nearly dark when Lex fired up the Cub and took off for home.

The steel clad container of human generated "honey" was soon covered by drifting snow, then with the spring thaw, it disappeared from view, never to be seen again. But, it was not to disappear from the people's memories or stories.

Lex, like all of us, sometimes missed critical things and occasionally did an inadequate pre-flight, but he was a very skilled, safe bush pilot.

It's a blessing when in spite of our grievous imperfections and peculiar peckadillos we survive to fly another day.

Landing Sites

O
ver a prolonged period of time, perhaps during the first flight, but more likely during the first several dozen flights or so, one who flies in rural Alaska will find it advantageous or even necessary to land in a place other than a maintained airport. In bush or rural country, the frequency of such off airport landings tends to increase and the quality of the landing site decreases with the passage of time, the pilot's experience, and of course, the circumstances. Gear types vary with conditions and range from small tires to large ones, from skis to floats, and combinations of the different landing apparatus. So it is with active bush flying.

In my case I began flying at Port Alsworth on Lake Clark, with the venerable master bush pilot, Babe Alsworth, as my unofficial instructor. The first airfield from which I took off and landed was the dirt and gravel strip at Babe and Mary's home. Not long after I began flying, Babe explained some of the things to be aware of on beach and hilltop landings. Then we went out and did some wild country landings in his Piper Super Cruiser (PA12).

In 1969 I enrolled in an approved flight school at Merrill Field in Anchorage called Pat's Flying Service. The G.I. bill paid for the school. The instructor quickly realized that I already had some experience and cut the tail off my shirt after less than three hours of dual instruction. I took the written test and had my Private Pilot license in hand. I was officially an honest to goodness pilot! My instructor slapped me on the back and congratulated me on having my "privates," but I assured him that had been the case since my birth.

In 1970 I purchased my first airplane, which was a 1959 Cessna 180, equipped with Federal wheel/skis. Only three hundred and five aircraft of that model were made in 1959. I paid the asking price of ten thousand five

An intended landing in "pucker brush" to access a remote area.

On 850 tires at our homestead strip with a moose.

On wheel/skis on international ice not far from Wrangle Island.

hundred dollars for the machine. With me having less than seventy hours logged, that airplane was too much for my experience, but by good advice, luck, prudent decisions, and the grace of God, I did gain experience and proficiency without having to do so by way of an accident with the Cessna.

The Cessna was used primarily for transporting me and my dental gear throughout Alaska from Barrow to Bristol Bay and Valdez and a total of fifty-seven communities that had no local private dentist, but I used it for personal pursuits as well as transportation in my developing guide service, as well. It was all invaluable experience and sometimes a lot of fun.

It's virtually impossible to own an airplane in bush Alaska and not use it for most every endeavor in which one engages. Roads are few and the weather is often cold and/or bad. Aircraft have made reasonable access to the bush not only possible, but practical for those who practice safe flying.

My 1959 Cessna 180 performed well and allowed me to do almost everything I cared to attempt … including some things that I had never dreamed I might do. But new STOL (Short Take Off and Landing kits were available and after owning my 180 for two and a half years, and flying a similar model with the cuffed leading edge and other, less significant modifications, I decided to have a Mid America STOL installed. The

An emergency extraction while on an autumn fishing trip.

Our lab, Zeke, and me with a nice catch of sheefish and burbot.

improvement on its already superb performance was remarkable. I resolved to never again own a standard Cessna 180, after seeing what a difference the STOL kit made.

————◉————

The Cessna allowed me to go places and do things and that never would have been possible for me without the flying machine, but I longed for an aircraft with an even better short take-off and landing capability. A Piper Super Cub seemed the inevitable choice. After less than three years of owning the Cessna, I purchased my first Cub. Once again, and with the able assistance of my friends and mentors, I lucked out and bought the best performing Super Cub that I have ever flown. As I write this, more than forty-two years later, I still own and fly that little airplane.

Three years later, I sold the Cessna and added a second Super Cub to the inventory list. I could keep one on wheels year 'round and use the other on floats during open water season and on skis during the cold times.

I made it a point to carry forceps, elevators, sutures and anesthetic—dental tools—along with aircraft tools at all times and most local folks knew it. I often did a little pro bono emergency work which ranged from removal of painful teeth to suturing of wounds on people and dogs while out and engaged in other pursuits. I used an "open air office."

Admittedly, I got a special thrill from the first several dozen solo flights, but that soon passed and in a short time I considered flying to be similar to riding a saddle horse. It was fine, enjoyable and all, but it was primarily a means of transportation … it was nothing like love. I do not recall ever going flying just to be flying. I always had a specific purpose. Most times I had multiple purposes for the trip.

While I had only an Assistant guide license I found part time seasonal employment with several independent Registered Guides. By guiding I could spend more time observing, stalking, harvesting, and preparing animals than I could ever devote to such activities if I did not assist others in their quests. It was not a question of money. I could earn much more money rendering dental services than I could make at guiding, but I became a dentist primarily so that I would not have to sell all my time to make a living. That dental degree and state licenses were permits

On a mountainside in the Wrangel Mountains with Jim Cann.

for me to live the life I had chosen and dreamed of since I had just emerged from infancy. The dental diploma was a lifetime hunting and fishing license.

In the late 1960s I would drive Jim Cann's 1955 Chevy pick-up from Anchorage to Chitina. From there he flew me in his Super Cub with the camp gear to Skolai Pass where I set up the camp. Then he would bring in the hunters in pursuit of Dall sheep and the occasional black bear. Two months after I purchased the Cessna 180, I began flying my airplane, loaded with gear and supplies, to either Chitina town or Jake's Bar on the Chitina River. Jim would ferry me and the gear on to the Pass in his Cub. We used this system for the next several years.

Sunlight and anything from rocks to bushes or even material intentionally dropped from the aircraft to mark an area, give the pilot a sense of depth and perspective and are invaluable aids when landing in the bush. Without either good light or clear markers of where the hard ground and the often nebulous air above interface, the landing should not be attempted. An early August snowfall in the Wrangel Mountains in the preceding picture illustrates such a successful landing in a hazardous location. If not for the black rocks showing through the new snow, we would not have landed in that place at that time.

Most of the gnarliest places I wound up landing in were not photographed, as I had either too little time, too little light, or camera problems.

Wolf control efforts often led me to land on hillsides and mountain tops.

A wolverine bonus from a caribou survey flight. The shadows in the photo indicate it was late on a spring day, but light enough to distinguish and avoid the swales and lumpy areas.

I experimented with cameras that had self timers, with mixed results.

A bit narrow and curved, but adequate for a Super Cub or Cessna 180.

Often I was alone and just plain forgot to make a photo.

Several times, especially when flying between Kotzebue and Fairbanks or Anchorage I got into weather that was uncomfortable, to say the least. Most any road beats the average bush landing strip and I did make use of roads and trails on many occasions.

One summer in July I had a contract with the National Oceanic and Atmospheric Administration (NOAA) to fly the coast from Cape Prince of Wales through Kotzebue Sound and on up to Cape Lisburne. Our mission was to count the number of dead walrus we found on the beaches, and to land to determine the cause of death of those that were reasonably accessible. We were to take samples to allow NOAA's laboratory personnel to perform necropsies.

Nearly all of the dead walrus were headless. Obviously they had been shot and decapitated during the spring migration, some two to four months earlier. The carcasses emitted a unique odor, quite unlike any other that I had sensed.

This was a typical, expensive, federal government boondoggle. Well, it may not have been so expensive compared to other federal ill-conceived projects, I suppose, but beyond the counting of carcasses, it served no useful purpose. Necropsies ... what a ridiculous procedure to be performed on a headless walrus!

Anyway, we experienced dense fog that whole month. The thick stuff

Another set of ivory from a walrus wounded in the spring slaughter.

One of several carcasses that still had a head.

would roll in and hang over Kotzebue, giving visibility from zero up to a quarter of a mile -maybe, but the heavy blanket of blah abruptly ended just about a mile east of town—we experienced those conditions day after day. I would load the Cub with the NOAA investigator in the back, sit on the runway until we got a slight improvement, get a special clearance to depart and bore up through the soup, which was usually only five hundred feet or so, then fly VFR on top to either Cape Espenberg or Cape Krusenstern—or any other place where there was decent visibility, and from there I would reduce altitude and begin searching the beaches.

Each year we counted over two hundred and fifty headless walrus carcasses between Cape Prince of Wales and Kotzebue, even though we could not survey the beaches south of Kotzebue for more than ten miles due to the fog. For each carcass, I would land, then walk over to assist in taking the samples. Often we could reach several carcasses from a single landing.

For walrus carcasses still in the water, I would wade out if necessary (I usually got soaked early on each effort, so I stayed wet all day), attach a three eights inch nylon rope to the animal, run it through a ratchet come-along and anchor the free end to the gear strut of the Cub. Just a little constant pressure on the carcass allowed the surf to move it closer to the beach. I made continual adjustments to maintain tension on the rope and after a short time we could access the foul smelling biomass.

At first the NOAA man used a chain saw to decapitate the few walrus that still carried heads and ivory, but soon I convinced him that a sharp butcher knife was simpler, quicker, and less messy to use for the beheading job. Furthermore, it was much simpler to clean after use. I used rubber hip boots and a pair of rubber gloves for the putrid sample collections.

On some of the more easily accessible and fully beached carcasses, I removed the oosik, or penis bone—also called a baculum. Upon returning home, I placed the smelly parts in one of the twenty foot vans I owned. In summer time, flies laid their eggs and the maggots cleaned up the putrid pieces pretty thoroughly. By freeze up time, the smell was reduced and the heads were cleaned up very well.

The oosik is composed of especially dense bone, similar to that of the mandible, or lower jaw bone of a walrus, and the hard surface took a high polish well. I gave or traded many of the salvaged oosiks to local

Eskimo carvers who etched them or made cribbage boards from the uniquely interesting bones. And I swapped some oosiks to people for various treasures.

The government contract called for counting the walrus and collecting tissue samples from all the dead ones we could get to, but the NOAA guy wanted to take all the ivory he could. Where the tusks eventually went, I never did learn. We were limited by weight, the condition of the beaches, and the compromised circumstances under which we operated, so three walrus heads was the maximum I would allow him to take back in the Cub each day. Most days we did not find that many walrus that still had heads.

For years before and after that NOAA contract I salvaged walrus heads and oosiks from beach wash-ups. Shortly after the contract was completed, that same summer, I flew back over the beaches following westerly wind storms and recovered still more ivory. It was a stinky, but interesting line of work. An appropriate chore for a dentist, I suppose some would say.

One never knows what the wind and weather may bring. Our official forecasters do the best they can with what information they have, but as we all know, their predictions and guesses are often wrong. Snow can come any month of the year in the far north, and it sometimes comes in large doses.

When one is stuck out in the bush with too much snow to land or take-off, the most sensible thing to do is just patiently wait until the white stuff melts off or melts down enough to permit safe ground operations. Having enough food and toilet paper is a good idea, as well as an interesting book or two.

It's always a good idea to sweep snow from the wings and control surfaces, rather than let it accumulate, but packing a runway can lead to problems as the packed snow sometimes quickly turns to ice, making braking difficult to non-existent, and prolonging the bad runway conditions.

Herring Spotting

Fish spotting has become a common endeavor and Super Cubs are the most popular aircraft for this operation. While I was commercial herring fishing with Tom Dooley on his seiner, the *F/V REBEL*, we loaded the spotter plane atop the pile of seine web on the stern of the boat. It was extra work

Spotter's Super Cub loaded on the *F/V REBEL*.

A surprise August snowfall in the Arctic.

for the boat crew, but it provided a huge margin of safety to the aircraft, as well as comfort and convenience to the pilot and his back seat spotter. With an empty weight of between one thousand and eleven hundred pounds, the little Cub was no problem to lift and set in place with the main boom of the boat. Of course the aircraft was tied down to prevent it from slipping off the vessel.

For overnights and short periods the Cub remained nestled on the seine web and tied down to the boat, but in rough conditions and for most longer moves to different fishing areas, the Cub was flown and plucked out of the water when conditions permitted.

In previous seasons, Dooley's spotter plane had been a Cessna 180, which he also loaded on the stern of the boat, but considerably more time and effort was required. Clearly, Super Cubs were the spotter plane of choice.

Breather Tube Problem

I purchased my first Piper Super Cub from a fellow in Anchorage in April of 1973. The aircraft was clean with relatively low time. It had been flown regularly, year-round, by the previous owner and it had never been wrecked. I flew it up to Kotzebue and put it to immediate use, flying it twenty-five to fifty hours each month.

During the long Thanksgiving weekend of 1973, a friend named Don had asked that I take him moose hunting. Up to that date, no moose with antlers sixty inches or wider had been taken in the Kotzebue area and my buddy wanted to be the first person to harvest such a large trophy.

The previous August a local hunter had taken a bull still carrying velvet that he said had a sixty inch spread, but I was able to put a tape on the rack. It was a beautiful, symmetrical set of head gear, but it was only fifty-six inches in width. Had the metal tape stretched?

Later that month, one evening as I flew home from the cabin I spotted a big bull browsing on short willows only a few hundred yards from a suitable gravel bar that I could land on. I convinced myself that it would go over sixty inches and we had yet to take a moose for our winter meat, so I landed and after a quick and easy stalk, I had the bull on the ground. I dismembered the moose, leaving the hide on the four quarters, before packing the back straps, tenderloins, heart and antlers to the plane to take home. I came back the next day for the meat of the four quarters and the ribs. (Until 1974 it was legal to take moose the same day airborne and one could legally remove and transport the antlers before the last of the meat was taken out.)

After I had the last of the meat home I took time to put a tape to the antlers. The spread was exactly fifty-nine inches. It was a good thing I was hunting alone, as I would have bet anybody some heavy dollars that the bull was destined to be the first sixty incher taken in North West Alaska. And I would have lost my money!

On the morning of our late November hunt, the weather was clear and cold with overnight lows in the minus twenty degree range, so I had used a catalytic heater to keep the engine warm enough to start. I had the Cub on Landis 2500 skis, tied down on the sea ice about two hundred yards from my house.

Sunrise came around noon-thirty (clock time) and we departed just as the first rays of light were breaking over the horizon to the east of town. Still loosing about eight minutes of sun per day, we had about three and a half hours of daylight in which to do our deed. So long as the sky remained cloudless, I was not worried about returning after sunset as the bay surface was smooth and I had been using the same ice strip for more than a month.

We flew directly to a series of large lakes about thirty minutes north of Kotzebue where I had taken a meat bull in 1969. Sure enough we eyeballed eighteen adult moose in the vicinity, and four were large bulls. Better still, one of the bulls was clearly sporting the largest set of head gear, and I was sure he would measure over sixty inches in width.

Although the biggest bull did not have the most esthetically pleasing set of antlers, his impressive width made him Don's chosen target.

A long narrow lake offered me an ideal place to land and it was separated from the moose by something like three hundred yards, which included two small stands of trees which would conceal our advance. We should be able to approach the animals to within easy shooting range.

But the snow was deep and soft, so our progress was laborious and slow. Nevertheless we snowshoed our way to within one hundred yards of the animals, waited until the widest one offered a clear shot, and after three rounds from Don's .270, the big bull was down.

With the precious daylight soon to disappear, we worked quickly to remove the four legs, followed by the back straps. We each packed a hind leg to the plane, then returned for me to take the back straps and Don a front leg. I placed the four loads of meat in the Cub and told Don to use the ax to remove the top set of ribs, pare out the tenderloins, set the heart aside, and chop free the remaining set of ribs. Then he could cut or chop

My buddy and his family with the 64 inch moose rack.

the head free of the carcass and make as many trips to the landing lake as he could. I told him I would be back in a bit over an hour.

I reminded Don that with the cold conditions, any meat we didn't get out that day would keep fine. I would return in the morning to get it.

In town I rushed to transfer the meat from the plane to my sled and jumped right back in to retrieve Don and as much of the rest of the moose as possible.

When I landed I was expecting to see one load of meat at the lake and my buddy close by, packing a second load. But no load was at the lake and Don was about midway from the kill site carrying the antlers.

When he arrived, he told me that he had trouble removing the head and he had not chopped free either side of ribs.

By then it was nearly sundown, so I tied the antlers on the right wing struts and we headed for town. It was not an ideal situation, but the remainder of the moose would keep overnight with no problem. Once tied down, I re-fired the catalytic heater, placed it inside the cowling, and called it a day.

The next morning was a carbon copy of the last, so after a five minute warm-up I took off. Before I had climbed a hundred feet, a large streak of oil came out of the back of the cowling and raced up my windshield. I made a turn and landed. The inside of the cowling was covered with oil. I found the "O" ring on one of the oil return lines had popped out and had slipped midway down the line, but it was still intact.

After some time searching, I located a hung-over mechanic wadded up in a broom closet at the hotel. After pouring some hot coffee down his throat, he agreed to look at the engine. He assured me it was a simple fix. I needed to buy a tube of Permatex, then get a large Herman Nelson heater, build a canvass tent over the cowling, and heat up the engine. He would be drinking coffee at Shellabarger's airport shack, ready for me to pick him up to reseat the "O" ring.

When all was ready, he coated the "O" ring with permatex, slid it up the line and popped it into place. That repair lasted until the engine swallowed a valve on cylinder number two in July, 1976.

But why had I developed the problem? The terminal end of the crankcase breather tube had frozen, making it non-functional and causing excessive pressure to blow the ring. The remedy was to punch a small hole in the breather tube about sixteen to eighteen inches up from the lower end, to allow the breather to function if the end of the tube froze. It was a simple after-factory modification necessary for cold weather flight.

That engine had flown for years in all sorts of weather and temperatures with the breather tube functioning fine. The mechanic told me that all the local fliers had punched similar holes in their breather tubes.

Breather tubs come from the factory without the hole, so all cold weather fliers should be sure to modify the breather tube.

Is He Gonna Make It?

After I had owned my Super Cub, N3421P, for several years I was feeling very comfortable handling that little airplane. A few near misses had taught me a lot. I was very thorough with pre-flight inspections, careful about giving the engine plenty of time to warm up before taking off, and I went through each hundred hour inspection, and the annual with the mechanic, doing most of the work myself. Not only did I save a lot of money in mechanic's wages, but I gained first hand knowledge and confidence that everything had been attended to properly. I also picked up a lot of practical information on aircraft maintenance and basic mechanics. My own check list was more thorough than any mechanic's list that I had seen.

It is imperative that flying anywhere should be done with caution, beginning with the on-ground preparations. Flying in the wilderness with few roads or adequate runways has additional potential dangers to be avoided.

Back in the days when taking caribou the same day one was airborne was legal, I sometimes flew a single guest hunter out in search of animals that we might land close enough to stalk. On one such flight we had departed an alluvial fan and were headed back to the lodge, which was only about thirty minutes away. We lifted off and turned for home, but as I reduced power to cruise at twenty-three hundred rpms, the engine coughed and dropped to two thousand rpms. I pulled carburetor heat which caused a further reduction in power. I was expecting a surge of power as the heat cleared the carburetor of ice and I left the heat on longer than usual. I glanced at the fuel floats and saw that both tanks were approximately half full, but I switched from the left main to the right main fuel tank. There was no change in the rpms. When I removed carb heat I was still able to get only two thousand rpms. I checked both magnetos, but got no increase in power. Something else was drastically wrong.

Fortunately we were not heavy and had no need of gaining much more altitude. As we flew along, the rpms dropped to eighteen hundred. I was concerned that we might see even more loss of power.

My passenger was aware of what was happening and asked if we would be able to make it to the lodge. I told him that I figured we could, but in the meantime, there was nothing to do but keep heading that way. There were no adequate alternate landing spots. Oh, I could probably land without injury to my passenger or myself, but not without damage to the plane and most certainly we would not be able to take off from such a place.

About that time my passenger began singing a currently popular tune whose lyrics went "Is he gonna make it, we'll find out in the long run."

I didn't need that joshing at the time, as we were in an uncomfortable situation. When we were within sight of the lodge he tuned up again, and louder this time. He seemed to be entertained by the drama of our circumstances. I was not enjoying the situation in the least, but we were still in the air. We were flying at about one hundred fifty feet above ground level at reduced speed and I was unable to climb higher.

With a wind of about fifteen miles per hour coming from down the valley, I elected to land with a tail wind, rather than spend the extra minute or two which a go-around for a landing into the wind would require.

We got on the ground at the runway and the engine shut down completely before we could taxi into my tie downs. We were both happy to be pushing the Cub the short distance to tie it down securely.

I felt lucky ... no, more accurately, I felt blessed.

After a cup of coffee and serious contemplation I began looking for the source of the malfunction. Both wing tanks had plenty of gas and neither of their fuel sumps showed any trace of water. I began disconnecting the fuel lines piece by piece, beginning with the left main tank. I blew through the sections of line and found there to be no obstructions or restrictions. The main gascolator showed only clean gas. The fine brass screen separating the incoming fuel from the glass settling bulb was intact and clean.

That was as far as I had been with the fuel lines on a Super Cub, but one last short section of line ran into the carburetor, so I removed that as well. I found a small finger screen which was almost completely plugged with tiny, hair-like, filaments of what I later determined was chamois. Apparently someone in the past had used a chamois filter with the skin inside out. Tiny bits of chamois leather had accumulated in the line and finally enough reached the screen to partially block the fuel flow. That use of an inverted chamois must have taken place years before, as I was always careful to place the chamois with the skin side up. After that, I always checked the finger screen on every hundred hour and annual inspection, which is not routinely done by mechanics.

In the more than thirty years since that day, I never again found anything in that screen.

First Engine Failure

In 1976 the Alaska Department of Fish and Game (ADF&G) planned
to start the annual caribou census from No Luck Lake on the North
Slope. It was much closer to the calving grounds than Cape Thompson
where we were based in 1975, and it had a very snug cabin owned and
maintained by the Naval Arctic Research Lab (NARL), which we could
use. (See Bear Buggery story in my book: *Alaska Tales: Laughs and Surprises*.)

This census effort included me and one other chartered Super Cub and
one Cessna 185 flown by a state biologist.

We were landing with wheels on the ice of the lake, most of which had
been blown free of snow. Each day we would fly out to our assigned sector
to look for bands of caribou, returning to the base before midnight—or so
we planned. We left our flight plan posted in the cabin each day. In June, in
that latitude we had continuous daylight all twenty-four hours of every day.

I flew with the Nome biologist, Karl Grauvogel, in the back seat of my
Cub. We spent the first week in low level, slow flight with wing flaps down
looking closely at the rumps of cow caribou. We were checking for signs
of retained placentas, a condition which would lead to the death of the
cow, and then of course, her calf. Like most animals, caribou cows do not
adopt orphaned calves. If the cow dies, so does the calf.

Vitamin C deficiency can cause the placenta to not be released in normal
fashion after birth of the calf and ADF&G was intent on establishing if
that might be a factor in the recent large drop in the caribou population.
We and the other teams that were surveying sighted no retained placentas
in several weeks, and hundreds of hours of careful, close observation.

When caribou were in a mountainous area, to check their back sides
closely, the procedure was to fly to the higher terrane, then fly back down

Looking for retained placentas.

country for a close look, so we were flying into lower elevations, rather than having to climb.

This type of flying is extremely tiring, both for the pilot and the observer. The terrane is at best uneven and at worst precipitous—sometimes perilous. Even with minimal wind, thermals build up in the long sunlight of the ever lengthening days and create local turbulence.

The ice on all the lakes was beginning to "candle up." Vertical stands of rotting or melting ice softened the top, giving it the appearance of candles, and eventually leading to "rotten ice" and giving way to open water. The snow pack was melting rapidly, producing runoff water which swelled the streams. Flooding was rampant throughout the area.

We had decided that as soon as the flooding subsided sufficiently, we would have to move our base to a suitable nearby river bar to avoid the risk of loosing an aircraft through the softening ice. The carcass of a federal government DC3 had become part of the landscape on the south shore of No Luck Lake due to a bad landing and rotten ice some years before.

After more than a week of our vagina ... or "snatch watch" patrols, Karl suggested one morning that we fly directly to Cape Lisburne to check on

Three survey planes and a government wreck.

a band of transplanted musk oxen. His said his eyes and nerves would welcome a change of venue. I enthusiastically agreed and took the Cub to thirty-five hundred feet elevation as we headed west from No Luck Lake.

We were about thirty miles out of camp, crossing the head waters of the Utukok River. We had flown by that area the evening before at low level and noted that the river had overflowed its banks and was well up into the riparian willow patches. The water was flowing swiftly enough to bend over and wobble the bushes.

About two miles west of the Utukok my engine abruptly made a different noise, then a loud clatter, and oil came streaming out of the cowling and covered my windshield. I'd not touched the throttle, but my rpms dropped from the cruise setting of twenty three hundred to eighteen hundred. The Lycoming was making abnormal, alarming noises and I could not get more rpms, even with full throttle.

Something Was Seriously Wrong

The engine was a narrow deck 0320, one hundred and fifty horse power Lycoming and was due for an overhaul soon. I had a brand new engine rated at one hundred sixty horsepower in the warehouse in Kotzebue and had discussed installing it the week before when we were doing the Cub's annual inspection. The mechanic advised me to delay hanging the new engine until after the North Slope project, as the new power plant was more apt to give me problems than my high time, but tried and true, old engine.

That discussion and decision came to mind as I debated my options with my engine rattling and our altitude decreasing.

It was certain that I could not make it back to the lake with the seriously reduced power. I was wondering how long it would be until the engine shut down completely.

I banked left and headed for the Utukok, telling Karl that seemed to be our best bet.

Karl reminded me that the flood water was extensive in that area, but I told him that a flooded, relatively flat bank was preferable to the tundra tussocks, some of which were two to three feet high. We steadily lost altitude.

Soon I could see my intended landing spot and figured we could make it. Had we not been at thirty-five hundred feet when the engine malfunctioned, we would have been in a real bad way. Had it happened on any of the past ten days or so, we probably would have hit the ground beneath us in less than a minute.

Oil kept streaming over the windshield and the engine's clanking noises grew louder. The wind was blowing about ten to twelve miles per hour from the south.

As I approached the spot I realized that I would have to land with the wind on the tail, as I would not be able to make the landing place if I flew downwind and turned to land properly, into the wind. I told Karl to firmly grasp the overhead tubing to brace himself and to expect that we would likely flip over onto our back as soon as we hit the water.

I had to slip the plane to bleed off a little excess altitude to avoid overrunning the strip. Then as I pulled full flaps I saw that the area was no longer under running water. It looked like only shiny, wet mud was covering the bank. I cautioned Karl again to hang on and be braced for a flip.

There was no time for me to dread the touch down, it was coming up too fast. I lined up on a straight section of the easterly bank and committed

Note mud on the wings and oil on the belly.

us to land. I'd trimmed the Cub full nose up, so I had to relax the forward pressure on the stick as the three wheels touched simultaneously.

The sickening kersploosh of the contact was followed by the sound of mud and pebbles hitting the underside of the wings. One more small bounce and we were stopped. We were right side up with the greasy side still down. What a relief!

The "strip" was composed of firmly packed, stream polished gravel overlaid by four to six inches of mud and silt. The inboard portion of the wings, the tail feathers and the fuselage had several pounds of mud on them. The tail wind had not adversely affected us and I was ecstatic! We were safely on the ground with no injuries and no damage to the airplane, except for the engine.

We both got out of the Cub and I suggested to Karl that he look for a decent place to put up the survival tent. A dry place would be nice if possible, but if not, we'd cut some willows to put down and cover them with a tarp before setting up the camp.

I opened the cowling and saw oil all over the inside. That quick look was enough for the time being. I had that brand new engine in town and it was only a matter of time before we would be found and best of all, the plane was not damaged!

We unloaded the Cub and pushed it into the willows to secure it and clear the area for a rescue plane to land. I used orange surveyor's tape to mark off the best landing area.

A small esker (a lineal elevation of soil pushed up by a glacier) just off the strip provided us with a reasonably dry surface to set up our tent, and in a short time we had the single burner Coleman stove going and were enjoying hot chocolate and sandwiches for lunch.

A few caribou were straggling by and I suggested to Karl that we shoot one, just in case we wound up spending some serious time before being "rescued." He voted a firm "NO" to that idea. I warned him that if things got too hungry, there in the wilderness, I might wind up eating him.

Karl snorted.

Then I told him that he actually had little to worry about, as I reckoned he would be much too hard to clean, prior to cooking and consuming.

Karl grunted.

The engine had blown out nearly all the oil, but it was still turning when we landed. It was time to get the engine ready to remove while the weather was nice. An old abandoned government fuel dump was nearby from which we salvaged some gasoline boxes and other useful items for the engine exchange procedure.

I removed the cowling, then the propeller, stowed them safely in the willows, and began to disconnect the damaged engine.

The wind slackened and the sun worked at drying out our strip. We spent an enjoyable evening in our unintended camp and dozed off to sleep long before the brief Arctic twilight arrived.

Midmorning the next day, I heard the high pitched whine of the three hundred horsepower engine of the Cessna 185. I called the pilot on my VHF radio, telling him that the strip was drying out fast. He could safely land there now, but giving it another day to dry would keep him from having to wash the mud off of his plane, as well as make his landing easier with improved braking. I also asked him to get word to Buck Maxson in Kotzebue to bring my new engine up on his next trip. Buck could land his De Haviland Beaver or an Otter on this stretch of river bank without difficulty.

We spent another leisurely day in the Arctic, Karl took pictures, I continued to disconnect cables and such from the engine to expedite

Disconnecting the electrical and fuel lines.

replacement when the new one arrived. I washed most of the mud off the Cub and tinkered around with inconsequential things, just to have something useful to do with the time. I had no book to read.

Then I nosed around the creek, looking for signs of gold, but found nothing other than some pretty river rocks.

We enjoyed watching Willow Ptarmigan roosters defend their areas from other males as we soaked up the sunshine. One pair of roosters really went at it and finally one bird seemed to surrender. Then the winner of the battle pecked a hole clear through the skull of the loser and killed it. That surprised both Karl and me.

When by mid afternoon the next day we had seen no sign of our "rescuers," I told Karl to be sure to save any salt and pepper or spices he might have, as I was trying to think of ways to prepare him for dinner.

"Jake, if you ate me, I would be sure to make you sick," Karl warned me.

"Karl, you do that already," I replied.

This entire experience served to further solidify our friendship which was already several years old.

About four o'clock that afternoon I heard airplanes. The dull lub, lub, lub of a single engine otter and the higher whine of the Cessna 185 indicated they were coming our way. The state plane landed first, then in came the freighter. Buck had my engine aboard and had thrown in a couple of old car tires, a short tripod with a chain hoist and an itinerant mechanic, who had just that week come to Kotzebue looking for work. Wow! What luck! I could replace the engine myself if necessary, but much preferred to have a professional inspect everything prior to the test flight.

The mechanic, John, and I had the busted engine off the plane in an hour and the new one attached to the motor mounts before another hour had passed. It took a couple of hours the next day to get the new engine all hooked up. I put in seven quarts of mineral oil (used to break in new engines) which Buck had thoughtfully included with the new engine and other stuff. The test run was normal and John suggested that I fly it around the strip. I said fine, but he should ride with me. I always like to have the mechanic ride along on the first flight. In case he screwed up, he'll be there to enjoy the excitement. He agreed to climb in and after the short flight we agreed that everything seemed to function perfectly.

A quick inspection and partial disassembly of my original engine revealed that cylinder number two had "swallowed a valve," but the motor could be put back into service after a major overhaul. However, it was the older model, with a narrow deck, and I decided that after getting it to Kotzebue I would give it to Johnny Alsworth, a younger brother of my deceased buddy, Leon. Johnny was trying to establish an engine overhaul business at Merrill Field in Anchorage. I did ship it down to him at Alaskan Aircraft Engines, refusing to accept the normal five hundred dollar "core" price for the broken engine.

In 1999, after my second mid-air engine failure, Johnny loaned me a high time engine belonging to his brother Glen, to get me through the season. That pay back, twenty-three years later, was genuinely appreciated.

It's hard to imagine how anyone having a mid-air engine failure could come out better than I had after making a forced landing in the wilderness nearly two hundred and fifty miles from the nearest town. I was lucky and I knew it, but more accurately, I had been once again blessed and I thanked God.

Winter Survey on the North Slope

In reaction to the great drop in population of the Western Arctic caribou herd which was noticed a couple of years earlier and finally acted upon in 1976, the Alaska Department of Fish and Game began to intensify their management efforts on caribou in Northwest Alaska. An accurate census and survey of the herd's movements were some of the baseline data that was initially sought.

It had been speculated that a significant number of WAH caribou were over wintering on the north slope and could be responsible for the lower census counts which were usually done just a bit north of the Brooks Range in June, after their spring migration north. Maybe the caribou had not really died off,—or so some optimistic souls hoped! Possibly—hopefully—large groups had split off to form new and geographically separated herds. A few reports came in that indicated some animals were, indeed, spending the winter on the "Slope."

Actually, caribou over wintering on the north slope is a common occurrence, as every year some smaller collections of caribou could be found in the far north, but with alarm bells going off and fears of a massive die-off, the situation warranted a thorough investigation.

So in mid March, 1977, I was chartered, along with another Super Cub and pilot to do grid transect surveys from the north side of the Brooks Range to the Arctic Ocean. We each carried a biologist in the back seat. A base camp was selected on the Utukok River, at a place called Driftwood. It was the same place where I had made an emergency landing in June, 1976 when my engine swallowed a valve. It was a wind-prone location, but nevertheless, a relatively nice place to use for a winter base camp.

Fifty-five gallon drums of aviation fuel were flown in by Buck Maxson in his single engine otter, along with a fourteen foot by sixteen foot canvass wall tent and two smaller sleeping tents. Food, two Coleman double burner cooking stoves, sleeping cots, and other basic camp gear was included in the freighter load. Two grounds people maintained the camp, preparing simple meals, sack lunches, keeping a pot of coffee or tea available, and doing what they could to keep the cook tent tolerably warm, as well as keep the biologists and pilots reasonably content.

A big arctic high pressure ridge, a common condition during winter, was keeping the weather clear, providing great visibility most days which is so important for effective aerial surveying. But it was cold. Most nights were dropping to minus thirty degrees or lower. In the far north, the spread between the overnight low and the high of the day is small—usually less than ten degrees. I had resolved to avoid flying in temperatures below minus twenty, but this contract would require an exception to that rule, otherwise the survey could not be completed.

I had installed an extra heat shroud over the engine's forward crossover manifold pipe to provide a second source of cabin heat. This additional heat source was connected to a flexible hose which was long enough to extend to the back seat. Its heat flow could be controlled independent of the main heater. The extra heater hose was used and appreciated every day, especially by the back seat passenger. Cubs are notoriously cold, and the passenger in the back seat sits in the most frigid part of the drafty cabin.

After leaving one or sometimes two catalytic heaters under the cowling, with a heavily insulated and snugly closed engine cover over the outside, the oil was still thick and sluggish when the time came to start in the morning, but as long as it will drip off the end of the dip stick, its warm enough to start the engine.

We had no electricity available.

One super cold morning I loaded our survival gear and the biologist in the Cub, removed the heaters and rolled up the engine cover, then stuffed it in behind the passenger. I went to the front of the airplane to turn the prop through an entire cycle, which is eight strokes. This action is performed as a practical kindness to the engine and also saves the battery a little on cold starts. I've always treated my equipment kindly and I've received similar treatment from my machines.

The biologist that I hauled for most of that brutal survey had sustained a severe hand injury as a child, resulting in the loss of two fingers, while playing with firecrackers. As I was turning the prop through, on stroke number seven, the engine suddenly fired and the propeller hit the back of my right hand, sending my mitten flying through the air.

Seeing what he thought was my hand being chopped off, the biologist leaned out the open clam shell door and vomited violently.

The engine had only "popped" once and luckily it did not start. I grabbed my immediately painful and soon to be swollen hand as I went to retrieve my mitten which had landed about 20 feet away. When I returned, the biologist looked far worse than I felt. He looked at me and I told him that my hand was still attached to my arm, but that I wanted to get a small ace bandage from the first aid kit to wrap it, as I could feet that it was already starting to swell. Privately, I wondered how many bones were broken and how difficult this would make flying the aircraft, as I used my right hand on the control stick. Most of all, I thanked God, that in fact my hand had not been chopped clear off.

I stuck a small bottle of aspirin in my pocket for easy access.

However, my Cub was well rigged and after adjusting the elevator crank to trim the plane (with my left hand), following takeoff, the aircraft could be controlled almost hands free. Of course I would need to grip the control stick with my right hand, but most flying at cruise did not require a tight grasp or much pressure on the stick. In a few minutes I got into the plane, and pushed the starter button, The engine turned over easily, started, and after plenty of time for a warm up, we took off.

As Murphy would have it, our route this day took longer than expected, putting us back at the tent camp just as twilight began to restrict visibility. The glare of sun on snow and ice all day long had been hard on my eyes and they were watering, which negatively compromised my vision even more than the diminishing daylight.

But the only accident that day was the one I had caused by carelessly leaving my magneto switch on Left Mag the night before. The Left is the impulse magneto and commonly used alone for more easily starting the engine. However both mags should always be turned off when the engine is shut down and left on OFF when turning the prop through or otherwise manipulating the propeller.

It was sheer neglect on my part that I had not completely turned the key switch off the night before, nor had I checked the switch prior to hand propping the engine. It was a lesson, the cost of which could have been much higher. Prior to turning the engine through by hand, both magnetos should be double checked and in the OFF position.

That evening I unwrapped the Ace bandage and was relieved to see my hand—though badly bruised and moderately swollen, was still functional. I could flex all my fingers and had a reasonably firm grip. Of course my hand was sore and hurt to move any part of it.

I'd been swallowing two aspirins every two hours or so to combat swelling and dull the throbbing pain. And Mr. Bayer's little white pills were working pretty well.

While at high altitude that day, I got off a radio message to a Barrow air taxi operator's pilot, who had relayed to the freighter pilot, Buck Maxson, my request to bring along a bale of fiberglas batt insulation from my warehouse in Kotzebue on his next supply trip to the camp. When the roll of Johns Manville batts arrived, we affixed strips of batts to the ceiling of the wall tent. The batts kept coming loose and required periodic replacing and re-taping, but the insulation remarkably improved the heat retention in the tent. All six of us slept in the big tent, which was the only one that had any heat source. We left all the burners of the two Coleman cooking stoves on all the time. It helped, but the interior of the tent remained uncomfortably cold.

I had slept much warmer and more comfortably in my emergency snow cave a few years before.

My hand, in spite of active use, improved daily. I have always been blessed with a high pain threshold and quick healing.

The survey resulted in a count of only a few hundred caribou which were scattered over the slope, with the largest group having only nineteen animals.

The low caribou count was disappointing, but not unexpected.

We did encounter a lone polar bear about 50 miles from the coast, which was noteworthy. It was not a huge bear, probably a three or four year old ice bruin.

The Otter and a load of supplies.

Winter camp, 1977 at minus thirty-five degrees. Wall tent in the background.

We found no wolves, but saw three wolverine, all singles, separated by miles of hard, windblown snow from each other. The stink bears were humping along, trying to make a living in that cold, hungry country.

This project took a little more than two weeks. I praised my bunny boots, dog skin mittens, home-made hooded, goose down parka with a wolf ruff, caribou skin mattress, sunglasses and good thermos bottles, among other things like … good luck and the blessing of not loosing my right hand.

We had none of the chemical heat packs which are so readily available today. We had no propane, kerosene or oil heaters for the tent—not even a small wood stove. We got some heat from the double burner Coleman camping cook stoves—the rest we generated ourselves.

Unlike some remote big game surveys, no one was sorry to see this one end. We took down the camp and saw the De Haviland Otter depart with the gear and camp attendants before flying back to Kotzebue for a long hot shower.

I'd seen colder temperatures in 1969 on a road trip to provide dental services to Dawson and White Horse in Canada's Yukon Territory. On my return trip I held clinics in Northway and Tok, Alaska, where it hit sixty-six below zero for two days. Now, that was so cold! I kept the truck running all night because I was concerned that, in spite of a large circulating water heater on the engine, it would not start if I let it sit too long. When traveling my dental assistant had to constantly scrape frost off of the inside of the windows so I could see to drive.

But, I believe that North Slope survey in March, 1977 was the longest period of intense cold that I have experienced without benefit of occasionally getting warmed up by a wood or oil stove, or better yet, a warm shower.

The North Slope of the Brooks Range is a tough place for man or beast to make a living, or to even just sustain life, especially in winter.

Caribou/Wolf Survey 1977

For the summer of 1977 caribou census, we based again at Driftwood, on a bank of the Utukok River, where I'd made my emergency landing with the bad engine the summer before and where we had based for the March, 1977, survey. This summer survey was scheduled to begin a bit later than in earlier years, in hopes that flood waters would have subsided enough for us to use a level section of bench land alongside the river for our landing strip. It turned out to be the best field base camp we had established.

We set up a large wall tent for cooking which also served as a communal meeting area and place to play cards in bad weather, of which we got a lot that year. Fog formed and hung in the low areas for days on end. It was damp and chilly the entire time we were there, that summer.

The strip was about thirty miles north of our lodge on Trail Creek and laid on a North/South axis, making it usually subject to cross winds but it was about as good as off airport landing strips get, by bush standards—when it was not underwater. One could accurately say it was as good as any and better than most bush strips.

Aircraft employed were my Super Cub and another Cub, and a Bell Jet Ranger helicopter which was primarily used for bear and wolf darting, followed by sampling and collaring of the predators. For a few days, the Alaska Department of Fish and Game had a De Haviland Beaver on big tires to use for taking photos of caribou which were later counted to arrive at an accurate census number.

Personnel in camp included a pilot for each aircraft, three biologists focused on caribou, a bear biologist, a wolf biologist, and the Alaska Department of Fish and Game's only entomologist. Occasionally some official visitor would drop in for a day or so.

By that time, which was the third year of concentrated efforts to obtain an accurate census, we had the habits of the Western Arctic Herd pretty well understood and mapped as much as was possible for those Arctic wanderers. Review of the extensive work done in preparation for the Cape Thompson "Project Chariot" in the late 1950s indicated that the meanderings of the caribou had changed little in the past several decades ... or perhaps centuries.

On days of decent weather our multiple aircraft forays monitored the gathering of the bands of caribou as we waited for the ultimate, maximum post-calving aggregations for the photo census.

When a grizzly bear or wolf was spotted, the information would be radioed to the helicopter while we kept track of the predator until the chopper arrived to dart it with a tranquilizer.

Once sedated, the animal was hoisted up on a tripod for weighing, the biologist always watched the animal for signs of overheating and, when necessary, dowsed it with buckets of water to keep it cool.

Once a bear was sedated and on the ground, a number was tattooed on the inside of its lower lip, a vestigial premolar tooth was extracted for age determination, blood was drawn and in some cases, a radio transmitter collar was placed. The general condition of the animal was noted and it was checked for external parasites, which are rare in Alaska. These procedures all took place in a few minutes. The helicopter crew stood by until the animal recovered, got to its feet and went on its way. On a few occasions, things got a little hectic with bears coming out of the sedation sooner than anticipated, but overall, the procedure was practiced and smooth.

One morning, immediately after we took off, my biologist observer, who I called Sasquatch due to his good nature as well as the size of his feet, spotted a large gray wolf close to the base camp. The chopper was soon hovering over it, the gunner darted it, and the wolf was on the ground. There was no place for me to land close by, so we went on flying in search of other wolves nearby. Finding none, we went back to caribou surveying.

That evening upon returning to camp, the wolf biologist, the helicopter pilot, and others were gathered around the wolf which was lying prone near the landing strip. It had not recovered from the tranquilizer, but was still alive, so they brought it to camp.

A biologist and me extracting a tooth from a tranquilized grizzly.

Sasquatch and I walked over to see what was up . The wolf man and pilot had their hands in the unconscious animal's mouth, which although it was not foamy, was plenty slathery with gin clear, slimy saliva. They were discussing how unusual it was to find a wolf with a willow branch stuck between its teeth! A willow branch of about one half inch in diameter was wedged between the space behind the upper canines from the right post canine diastema to the left. Sasquatch mentioned that might indicate that it was crazy and he wouldn't recommend playing with its spit. There had been no reports of rabies in wolves in that area, but the disease is endemic throughout mainland Alaska and is commonly carried by foxes.

That wolf did not recover and the biologists decided that keeping the head for rabies analysis might be a good idea. The head was sent to Kotzebue on the next supply flight. From there it was sent to Palmer for analysis.

When possible I would land the Super Cub close to the darted predator and assist in the ground operation.

I assisted some of the wildlife biologists in extracting the vestigial teeth which have conical roots. Those teeth were easy to remove intact with a dental elevator or a special forceps. The dental "tools" proved to be so effective, I ordered dozens of sets from a dental supplier, some of which the Alaska Department of Fish and Game are still using.

Weather was hindering our efforts, so we spent long hours telling jokes and stories. Eventually someone produced some playing cards. Poker with nickel, dime, and quarter limits was enjoyed by everyone. Then someone introduced us to a game called 727. In this game, cards had their number value, but face cards scored one half point and aces could be declared either one or eleven. With two cards face down the next card was dealt face up and bidding began. When no one took another hit, a final round of bidding was held before each player declared high which is 27 or low which is 7. The pot was split between the two winners. However, the perfect hand is two aces and a five. Anyone having that combination could declare high and low and win the entire pot. If the bidding is prolonged, due to even one player requesting another card, the pot can become large.

My Dad loved to gamble and told me that if you're not winning at least sixty percent of the hands, just fold up and go home, or at least leave the table, as you're luck is sour. After winning more than a fair share of hands that afternoon, I was dealt two aces in the hole and a five, face up. It was the perfect hand. One of the biologists, Karl, with whom I had shared the engine failure in 1976, had been loosing consistently and noticed that I took no hits and announced to all, "Jake is wanting everybody to think he has the perfect hand, but no doubt he's bluffing, as the other two aces are showing." Seven of us were playing and the pot grew large. Karl himself, had started off appearing to hold for low, but he prolonged the bidding and bumped the pot up by taking a few more hits, so, obviously he had switched his strategy and was going for high. Once a guy took a card, he had the option to place a bid, and on each occasion I raised the original bid to the maximum allowed. I had the hammer, and was using it on the other players. By the end of the play, the pot exceeded sixty dollars.

When the bidding stopped, before anyone declared, (declarations went round the circle and I was last in line, which is the most advantageous position), Karl said, "Jake, I know you're bluffing and I'll bet my rifle against yours on that." I warned him not to do that, but he insisted and added that he would take my rifle and when I had my next engine failure on the way home, a grizzly bear would really enjoy eating me alive.

I told him that was a cruel and unusual wish of his and I knew that it came from his stress and frustration, that he really wasn't such a mean guy, etc. My kindly, even fatherly, demeanor served to irritate him even more.

"You're bluffing, Jacobson and I'll make a side bet of $20 on it in addition to my rifle," Karl said.

Of course I advised him not to do it, adding that his children might go cold and hungry next winter if he had no rifle and was broke.

But those comments served to further provoke Karl, as I intended them to do. His face turned beet red. He would not be dissuaded and the bet was made.

Tension was evident in the assemblage in that tent as the wind blew and the rain continued.

Well, of course, I won the pot with that perfect hand. I had never been dealt one before and I never have since.

Karl stood up slowly, walked to his sleeping tent and brought back his rifle. I, with the most serious show of magnanimity I could muster, suggested that he keep the rifle until he got back to Nome. I could pick it up when I was down that way the next time, which would be in July.

Karl was actually quite upset. I intended to not take his rifle, but would not embarrass my friend with that admission in front of the others. The other guys joshed him, which hyped up his ire. Soon, he retired to his sleeping tent and tried to nap, but he laid awake, thoroughly disgusted.

On another foggy, miserable day, we had all been cooped up too long when I walked down to the river to get a bucket of water. In my pocket I had some bits of brazing rod that I'd melted and allowed to drop on some wet sand. They looked like gold, but were not as heavy.

However, everyone dreams of finding gold, especially when in bush Alaska. When, out of the corner of my eye I noticed Karl coming toward me, I dropped a few small nuggets into a clear shallow area of the river and deliberately picked one up as Karl came near, making sure he saw me looking at the "nugget" in my hand, I quickly thrust my hand into my pocket.

He asked me what I'd found and I replied "Oh, nothing, Karl"

He was hooked. He insisted that I show him what I'd put in my pocket and after making him swear to keep it a secret, I showed him the nugget. He immediately waded out to the spot and found several of the other "nuggets" I'd planted, then he waded out further into the current, totally preoccupied with his search for gold.

I went back to the tent and let the rest of the crew in on my little scam. (I'd been using this simple trick since before I was in high school and it seldom failed to hook my intended victim.) We all gathered on the river bank as Karl, once again my hapless victim, bent down to feel the bottom. His newly acquired toupee suddenly fell off and began bobbing its way downstream. Karl got thoroughly wet recovering that four hundred dollar hairpiece and we all had a good laugh.

When Karl climbed up the river bank with his toupee, I hollered that everyone should stay clear of Karl as he had Herpes ... hair piece. Karl did not laugh at that clever pun.

Over the next few days I saw him looking around the stream for more "nuggets" on several occasions. No one told him the inside story of the nuggets and he never caught on.

That same afternoon I decided to heat up a kettle of water and take a bath in the canvass wall tent I was sharing with the state's entomologist, an older, crotchety fellow of Scandinavian descent, named Ken. Ken was a bit coarse with his language around the females in camp and had a tendency to make his conversation sound more like orders than mere comments. His overall demeanor irritated some, but I felt like I knew his type and was not bothered. And Ken liked me, as I was "the only true Viking, in the lot," he said.

We all kept a large caliber pistol, shotgun or rifle handy for bear protection. Several times each summer grizzly bears had strolled right through camp, walking in between the closely situated tents. No camp bear was ever shot, but we were always fully on alert for them and normally tried to scare the sows with cubs away before they came too close. It was feared that a Cub would get into trouble or get frightened by the tents, gasoline drums or other material with which bears was entirely unaccustomed. If the Cub showed alarm by bawling or other means, it could lead to dangerous aggression from the sow. So, everyone kept a suitable firearm handy at all times.

There came an opportunity for me to bathe that afternoon. As I was bent over the wash basin, peeled of all my clothes, half shampooed and sudsed up, Ken threw open the tent flap to enter. Hearing the sudden noise, I grabbed my .44 Magnum revolver and wheeled around to face the danger with soap in my eyes, ready for a bear. When I recognized Ken's grizzled face I pulled back the hammer and shot into the ground near my feet where I had dropped my under wear. Dirt and pea gravel peppered the sides of the tent.

"Uffda, Jake, take it easy, you nearly gave me a heart attack," Ken gushed.

"Ken, you should be thanking me, as I may have saved your life," I said.

"Whaddu mean, saved my life," Ken questioned.

"Well, you came in without so much as a howdy-do and once I realized you were only a grizzled old coot and not a grizzly bear, out of the corner of my eye I thought noticed that my skivvies were moving. No telling what might be in them, after ten days without changing, so for your protection, I blasted them," I explained.

Ken sat down on the end of his cot and laughed so hard, the others in camp came on the run to share in the fun.

Luckily I had a towel handy or the ladies would have been subjected to an unintended flashing.

After about a week word came that the wolf had tested positive for rabies, so anyone who might have been exposed would have to take the dreadful series of shots. Those injections were given parenterally through the stomach muscle into the peritoneum and were known to be excruciatingly painful.

I flew one of the biologists that had foolishly exposed himself (only to rabies as far as I know—nothing perverted or anything like that!) to Kotzebue and as he was nervously sitting in the waiting room, I contacted a nurse and asked her to allow me to gown up with a head cover and a mask. I told her of the biologist's exposure to the rabid wolf and what I had in mind. She, being a friend and accustomed to my practical jokes, allowed me to do it.

We made up a concoction consisting of green food coloring from the kitchen mixed with water, with some coarse ground pepper thrown in, just for effect. It was a nasty looking mix.

The nurse ushered the poor guy into a small room.

Wearing a gown, a cap and a mask I approached the biologist with the largest syringe we could find, filled with the green liquid. When I entered, holding the huge irrigation syringe up high, I squeezed a little of the noxious appearing contents out the end of the needle—just like the real doctors do.

Our already distraught victim gasped and blanched, nearly fainting. I pulled the mask off and assured him that it was just a joke, but relieved as he was, he did not join the nurse and me in our raucous laughter.

To the welcome relief of everyone, no one came down with rabies.

For a couple of weeks we were joined by an attractive Norwegian female biologist who was collecting whole carcasses of caribou. She shipped them off to Fairbanks or somewhere for homogenization, followed by analysis for body composition of calves versus older caribou. The percentage of fat, protein and other components was to be determined by the laboratory. I was disgusted by the thought of homogenized caribou calves. Oh well.

All of the caribou antlers are in velvet that time of year and our Norsky lady biologist collected samples to analyze, study and ponder over, later, back in the lab. Asians were fond of making a tea out of reindeer antlers in velvet to serve as an aphrodisiac. As it turned out, there are high levels of testosterone in the antlers at that stage of growth. So maybe the tea really would be effective in putting some lead in their pencils. It was interesting watching her work.

That summer we were joined for a time by Frank and John Craighead, the famous grizzly biologists from Yellowstone Park. These brothers were true men of science, but very much down to earth and fun to be around. We all enjoyed listening to the stories they told. I believe they were pioneers in live capture and placing radio collars on grizzly bears in Montana and Wyoming.

One of the Craighead's sons was so taken with Northwest Alaska, he purchased a commercial salmon fishing permit and returned several summers to catch chum salmon for sale to dealers in Kotzebue. Chum salmon are also referred to as calico, dog or keta salmon. No doubt the name Keta was invented to give the fish a more appealing persona to potential human consumers. Who would want to eat a dog salmon, anyway—or your chum? The dog salmon that spawn and return to the far north are the best quality, and tastiest, of their species in north America. During their time in fresh water they do not feed. These fish have long fresh water river runs to make before spawning. Consequently their fat and oil content is much higher than that of salmon that do not have so far to travel for spawning. Fat and oil content give the Arctic dogs their superior taste.

When this long summer survey was completed, I flew the Kotzebue biologist, Sasquatch, back to town. We stopped at the Kelly River to catch some fresh arctic char and shoot some snowshoe hares for the table as well.

My friend Karl had flown his own Piper Super Cruiser (PA-12) up to the arctic camp and met us at the airport in Kotzebue. He offered his rifle to me, but I told him we'd had enough fun on that last hand of 727 and he should keep his firearm, as I didn't want any grizzly bear to eat him or his family to go hungry next winter. I had to rub it in a little. Karl joined us for supper and spent the night at my home.

When Karl saw the hares, he mentioned that they were scarce in the Nome area, so that evening after supper, Sasquatch and I skinned and gutted the dozen or so that we had taken, put the hides and guts in a large plastic bag and delivered the bag to the back seat of Karl's airplane while Karl was off visiting someone. Before he departed in the morning I gave him three hares, all butchered and packaged for him to take home.

As I got the story, Karl noticed the bag of guts, threw it in a corner of the plane's cabin and forgot about it. When he got to Nome, he was tired and did not unload most of the stuff in his airplane. About a week later when he went to his plane parked at the airport, he noticed a cloud of blow flies coming from the aircraft. He had not removed the bag of guts, but the flies had found it. He was not informed as to who had gifted him with the bag of refuse, which was just as well, as far as I was concerned.

We had some memorable times on those surveys with a great bunch of guys and gals. The work was interesting, made all the more so by the good humor.

More Winter Surveys

When I moved to Kotzebue there was just one permanent government dentist stationed in that small arctic town, then shortly after I set up my private practice in 1969, the United States Public Health Service (or Indian Health Service, as some called it) placed a second full time resident dentist in Kotzebue. The government dentists charged nothing for any services they rendered. This put me in a most unusual competitive disadvantage.

In order to survive if I wanted to live in that area, I needed to engage in multiple lines of work. I continued to fly to rural towns that had no private dental practitioner, and several native villages had persuaded the USPHS to contract with me to provide for their dental care, rather than send a government dentist. I was paid on a fee for service basis, with my fees set at the median fee for Anchorage practices. This proved to be far more acceptable, cost effective and all around better for the recipients of the government provided dental care.

Once I began flying commercially, I was getting frequent requests for charter flights. The Alaska Department of Fish and Game needed to do annual big game surveys which primarily dealt with assessing and counting the populations of the various species of wild game. Soon I was contracted to locate, record, photograph and sample the remains of wolf kills and various other biological and related projects. I enjoyed the work, had the time and the aircraft, so I was most happy to engage in those efforts.

Moose are most effectively counted during the spring season, when heavy snow has them "yarded up" in willow patches. Warmer weather allows the moose to disperse, and once leaves are on the plants, the big herbivores seem to disappear. So we did most of the moose surveys in March. I decided early in my flying career that I would not fly if the ground temperature was colder than twenty below zero. Super cubs are notoriously drafty and all machines break more easily in colder conditions. Some days in March were just too cold to fly, but we would usually get all the areas intended for survey completed by late in the month. We carried survival gear, a tent, sleeping bags, some food, a rifle, an ax, etc., but we usually made it back to Kotzebue or whatever base we were using, which was sometimes a tent, for the night.

Several factors can make a take off on skis difficult. Heavy, wet snow, wind direction, weight of the aircraft and occupants are all mitigating factors. Overflow water just beneath the surface of the snow is sometimes difficult, if not impossible, to see before you feel it on landing, and the water can seriously compromise both landings and takeoffs.

In late March of 1976, before we had a full time resident biologist in Kotzebue, the state (ADF&G) biologist from Nome, Karl Grauvogel, came up for a week of moose surveys. Karl and I had become friends and had put in hundreds of hours flying surveys together since our first meeting. As we were returning to town one afternoon after a long day of counting moose on the Kobuk River, I saw a large number of ravens rise up from a dense willow thicket near a lake. I banked the plane for a closer look and saw a moose lying in a brush patch surrounded by deep snow. But no tracks were near it, as would be the case if it was a predator kill. The biologist, Karl, wanted to check the carcass to determine why the moose had died. I told him that the snow looked soft and deep, and it was late in the day, but he insisted that we land, rather than take extra flying time to come back another day. A nearby lake provided reasonable access to the carcass. So I landed.

The touch down was soft—in fact a bit too soft—and the plane sunk past it's axles in dry powder snow. The "tail feathers" (elevators and horizontal stabilizers) were just above the surface of the snow. Had they been just inches lower, the fabric covering the elevators might have been damaged, especially if the surface of the snow was crusted. Since we were stopped and fully committed, Karl got out and quickly sank past his knees. As he tried to get to the carcass he was soon in snow over waist deep in the drifts near the edge of the lake. It was too late in the day to be fooling around with the temperature at minus eighteen degrees and forecast to drop to minus thirty overnight. It was going to be difficult taking off, but I gave it a try and had to chop the power when I couldn't get up to speed. The next

The snow was too deep to take off with my passenger.

best idea was for me to try to take off alone, then land on the river, which was about a half mile away, but blown free of most of the snow. Karl would have to battle his way to the river to be picked up. It was not a welcome prospect, but it was the best alternative, given the conditions.

My take off was not pretty, but I got airborne and flew to the river and then back to Karl to be sure that he knew where I would be waiting.

After landing, I opened the caribou skin sack that held my thermos, augmenting it's heat retention, and enjoyed the last cup of coffee as I waited for Karl to come busting through the willows at the edge of the river. When he did arrive, he was sweaty and tired, but relieved to be headed for a hot shower and a warm bed in town, at my house.

So we never did find out why that moose had died. New snow had drifted around the carcass and there was not enough time for Karl to dig around to properly investigate.

I reminded myself and Karl, that if the snow conditions look soft and deep, they probably are too deep for landing, especially with a passenger of Karl's size.

A Wolverine Beckoned

The thermometer indicated minus twenty-seven the following morning. That's colder than I normally operated, but the schedule for completion of the moose surveys was tight, so since my catalytic heater had kept the engine warm, we decided to take off for the Nimiuktuk River. Noatak was the only village between Kotzebue and our destination and was reporting minus fifteen degrees which was warm enough, so that encouraged us to go ahead with the survey.

Even with my regular and auxiliary cabin heaters set on full, we were cold from the outset.

The Nimiuktuk flows south from the peaks of the Western Brooks Range into the upper Noatak River. I had hunted on that drainage in all times of the year and learned that wolverines (*Gulo gulo*) in that area would often go up a cottonwood tree if they heard an airplane. We were sashaying back and forth up the "Nimi" counting moose which were in groups of two to twenty when I saw a small, well marked wolverine humping along the main branch of the braided river. As we approached the animal it immediately turned and climbed up a cottonwood.

A wolverine in a tree is an irresistible siren to most hunters and I had just acquired a mail order Army surplus thirty caliber carbine which I thought would work well on wolves and other fur bearers.

Karl had never seen a wolverine go up a tree before, so when I suggested that we take our lunch break then and there, he agreed.

Persuaded by the possibility of collecting that dandy fur, and feeling rushed for time, I did not evaluate the landing area as carefully as I should have done. I figured I needed to land as close to the tree holding the wolverine as possible, before the animal spooked and fled. The surface of the river had frozen up rough. After initially freezing, pans of ice had broken loose, piled up and refroze leaving abrupt ridges. Subsequent snowfalls had concealed some large bumps which I began to sense immediately after touch down. The banging of the landing gear became more noisy and the jolts more uncomfortable as the plane's velocity decreased and more weight was transferred from the airfoils to the main gear.

I jumped out of the Cub, grabbed my carbine and hustled to the tree with Karl close behind. I paused for him to take some photographs before I squeezed the trigger. The outside air temperature was minus thirty-five degrees.

I was shocked when the firing pin made a dull thud, but did not set off the primer. I tried several times, but no shot resulted. I was confident in the Army surplus ammunition, as I had test fired plenty of it earlier that winter. I told Karl to stand close to the tree and make a racket if the wolverine decided to come down. I ran the carbine to the plane, put it inside the engine cowling to warm the action and I placed the engine cover over the cowl. Then I got my short Hudson Bay ax (with a thirty-two inch handle) and returned to the tree. Karl was still clicking his camera as I began to climb up the tree. I was able to get part way up the tree, hoping to hit the critter in the head and stun or kill it. Before I could make my first swing, the wolverine, by then really irritated, came hissing and growling, down the tree toward me. I did not want that thing on me,- or down my neck, so I got down.

A new idea came to me. I told Karl to strike the tree with the ax if the wolverine tried to come down while I went back at the Cub to get the warmed rifle. He said he wasn't getting close to that tree. Darn, this was one of the few times that I did not have a .22 caliber pistol with me.

I got to the Cub, took the warmed carbine out and test fired it. It worked. As I hurried back to the tree Karl hollered that the wolverine was gone. Rats!

By then I was sweaty. Years before I had strengthened my Cub's axles with heavy steam pipe driven inside the hollow factory produced axles, but small cracks were showing at the weld on both of the axles, due to that rough landing. Again, Rats!

Clearly, it was time for Karl to take another walk. It was nearly a mile to a good lake with a smooth surface that I could land on—if I could take off from the rough river site without a wreck. Then if the cracks had not worsened, I would load Karl and we could continue the survey, planning no more unnecessary landings before we arrived back in Kotzebue.

I wrapped safety wire around the axles, hoping that would help prevent further cracking. I wrapped nylon reinforced tape over the safety wire. And I said a prayer.

Karl was slowly shaking his head, but he had enough good sense to see this was our most reasonable option.

We turned the plane around by hand and used the ax to smooth out the worst of the ice ridges. As Karl started off toward the lake I let the engine idle while I chopped ice to smooth out a path for my take-off.

I said another little prayer that the axles would hold. Keeping the stick back to remain nose high, to minimize weight on the main gear I gave it full throttle, wincing at each bump and dreading a gear collapse. Without Karl's two hundred and forty plus pounds of flesh, boots, and clothes in the back, I was airborne quickly and the skis appeared to be in their normal position—they were not cocked right or left and the tips were up, so I landed and carefully checked the axles as I waited for Karl. His shank's mare trip this day was longer, but less difficult than the one in the deep snow of the previous day.

He asked if I was sure the axles would hold as together, we inspected them. Nothing to do but try, I figured. Lucky for us, this lake was smooth with about three inches of good snow over the flat ice. Again I kept the nose high to reduce weight on the main gear and our take off was a text book, soft field procedure. I kept visually evaluating the alignment of the skis as we completed the survey of the drainage, but they held their normal position and looked good.

The landing on the sea ice in front of Kotzebue was after dark, but smooth. I did not gas up the plane, as I planned to replace both axles with spares from my parts shelf the next day.

Biggest Wolverine

The next day was windy, but warmer as I replaced both cracked axles. The damaged ones would be closely inspected, welded and kept as my new spares. The plane was ready to go by noon, but the distance to the survey site was too far for such a late start, so we held off. It was good to have a one day break from the stresses of cold weather surveying, anyway.

For the past couple of years, Mae and I had been taking in several wolverines along with our wolves for sealing by the state biologist, as was required prior to selling or even cutting them up for personal use. Most of our fur was taken by landing and shooting, which was legal at the time, but we got a few in our traps and snares, as well.

Karl had questioned me a time or two about how we got so many wolverines, I told him that with a little luck, I would get the opportunity to show him.

Mae with five wolverine and one wolf skin, ready for sealing by ADF&G.

We were counting moose on a branch of the Kobuk River again when I saw a huge wolverine humping along a hillside. I pointed out the animal to Karl and he said I could try for it, but he wanted to record the tachometer time as soon as I began the pursuit, as the state should not have to pay for whatever amount of flying time pursuing the wolverine might take. I agreed.

This wolverine looked big from the get go. He was on a slope too steep for me to use for landing, as it would put excessive stress on the downhill gear and risk causing it to collapse. As I was watching the animal, it turned up a little side swale that was gentle enough to permit a safe, slightly uphill, landing, so I set up and landed as close to the animal as I could. This time I had my 25:06 as well as my .22 pistol.

When the Cub stopped, I jumped out, Karl handed me the rifle and I took a shot and rolled the wolverine. Karl said "Well, Jake, I'm impressed," just in time for us to see the beast get up and start humping away. The second shot balled him up again. This time he stayed down.

Wolverine typically ball up into a tight fetal position when they are shot. I told Karl that this was the biggest wolverine that I had ever seen, and indeed, it turned out to be just that. We weighed it that night on my bathroom scales where it registered forty-three pounds, after loosing two or three pounds of blood. It was a huge male, and well marked. Karl never questioned me again about how I was getting wolverines.

My biggest wolverine—43 pounds

The Dead Cow Moose

It was late March about 1978 or so when I was flying a moose census on the northwestern aspect of Seward Peninsula. In the back seat, suffering from "Super Cub butt" after several days of survey flights, the new biologist from Nome was lamenting the fact that the number of moose seemed to diminish as we surveyed further to the west—toward the coast, and the villages. No caribou used that area, so the villagers depended on sea mammals and Arctic Hares, which are large "jack rabbits" that weighed up to seventeen pounds each. Muskox had been introduced, but were not yet well enough established to hunt.

Moose were expanding their ranges throughout northwest Alaska and a larger population in that area would certainly augment and compliment the local human diet. In the meantime, perhaps due to the overly lengthy hunting season which ran from August 1 through December 31, the animals were increasing, but at a very slow rate. A commonly discussed option was to reduce the season to promote an increase in moose numbers. Local villagers almost universally opposed that possibility. Most of the villagers took moose well after freeze up which normally took place sometime in October.

We were working our way down the Serpentine River drainage when we saw a moose lying in deep snow, not far from the river. When we got close, we could easily see fresh tracks of a snow machine pulling a sled which led up to the moose. Prints in the fresh fallen snow indicated the driver had got off the machine, approached the fallen moose, then departed. I climbed the Cub to about fifteen hundred feet and we could see a snow machine and sled traveling at great speed away from us and toward Shishmaref. It was hitting drifts and bouncing around wildly with the sled shifting from right to left. The driver was obviously in a big hurry. It appeared likely that he had shot the moose, heard the Super Cub, and got out of there.

The biologist wanted to pursue the machine and driver, but I reminded him that I was contracted only for biological work, which did not include pursuit of potential or even probable game violators. He reluctantly agreed, then insisted that we land near the carcass where I could eat my lunch while he investigated the scene.

So, I landed. Once again, the virgin snow was deeper and softer than I had anticipated, but at least we had a relatively straight take off run which appeared to be long enough for the conditions and load, and it was slightly downhill.

It was warm and calm in the winter sunshine as I enjoyed the lunch break.

Then I heard the sounds of snow machines coming our way from upstream. With the biologist still at the moose, three snow machines and riders, each pulling a sled came into view. I knew them all, and they all recognized my plane and cordially greeted me. One asked what I was doing, so I explained the survey and that we had noticed a dead moose, which the biologist was looking at. One man in the group observed that the snow was not so good for my take off and suggested that they pack a runway for me with their machines. I gratefully accepted. When the route was packed, they offered me a freshly killed Arctic Hare, which I also accepted. The biologist returned to the airplane and the snow machiners stood by as I loaded my passenger. I thanked each one as I prepared to take off.

Once in the air, the biologist told me that the moose was a cow pregnant with two calves and had obviously been shot by the first snow machine driver using .223 Ball (steel jacketed) ammunition which was used by the

National Guard units located in all the villages in those days. He had gathered a handful of empty shell casings and was anxious to follow the tracks to the village to make an arrest. I objected, so he said that as we had completed that portion of our survey area, we should fly directly to Kotzebue to enable him to call in the violation to the game warden in Nome.

It was disheartening to see the wasted cow with her two unborn calves. Too much of that sort of thing could delay or even prevent moose from reaching stable population levels in that area, to everyone's disadvantage. It was purely reprehensible behavior in any event.

However I did tell the biologist that I was certain that by morning the moose would be in the village, cut up and distributed, not left in the field to waste. I believed that had the shooter not heard my engine noise, he would have cut up the moose and loaded it into his sled, rather than flee the scene of the crime.

Still, it was a shame that the moose had been killed. It would have been far better if the cow had birthed and raised her calves, making three more moose in the area.

As soon as we landed in Kotzebue, the call was made to Nome. The following morning the game warden, one Sergeant Preston—yes, that was really his name, but he wasn't a Canadian Mountie from the Yukon—flew to Shishmaref and had little trouble establishing the identity of the shooter. An arrest was made after the suspect was mirandized.

I was uncomfortable with my position in this action, but I was not named by the state as a witness and the people from the village did not ever mention it to me, to my great relief, as I viewed them as friends.

After a few months a jury trial was conducted in the village, with the accused being represented by a Public Defender. The state spent a lot of money, but lost their case, to no one's surprise. It's unlikely that the lawmen will get a conviction when the juries are made up of relatives or close associates of the accused, and in this case, some or all members of the jury probably had enjoyed eating some of the meat of that same moose.

The following year the moose season was lengthened by another three months—to March 31.

So much for game management when the politicians get their hooks into it.

BLM Surveys, Lake Inventories

July, 1978 was the first time I flew a survey of more than a few days in duration for the Bureau of Land Management, or BLM. The contract called for me to fly the float plane from Kotzebue to Salmon Lake on the Seward Peninsula, where we would be based. I took my own four-person tent, sleeping bag and cot, loaded up the plane and flew in clear, calm weather straight across Kotzebue Sound to Goodhope Bay.

Once over land, I decreased my altitude to better enjoy the scenery. It was beautiful. I flew over the lava beds west of Imuruk Lake thinking of how some miners had followed the flow of ancient creeks, dredging the gravel as they went. When they came to the lava, they tunneled underneath, staying with the ancient creek's course, as they sought the placer gold. At least one such miner was still at it when he tapped an underground hot spring to provide heat for his home and other buildings.

Soon I could see the Taylor Highway easily marked by clouds of dust stirred up by a couple of passing vehicles. I located Salmon Lake and landed at the designated place, which was a small cove protected from the main body of the lake. The little cove made a good place to beach the heels of the floats of my small plane, protected from rough wind-driven water from the main lake. Stakes provided good anchors for my tie-down ropes.

Nearby I found the BLM fisheries biologist, Joe, and the camp cook, Hank, getting lunch ready.

After eating, Joe and I took off with some trammel nets, which are essentially a series of gill net panels hung adjacent to one another that had different meshes of netting. We were using five panel nets. This device caught everything that tried to swim through it, including sticklebacks and small fry of various types. The objective of the project was to inventory as many lakes as we could within range of the base camp to determine what species of fish were present and estimate population densities. We would set one net, then fly off and set two more. We tried to work three nets simultaneously. After soaking for a few hours, we would pick the nets, recording what we'd caught. In between setting and picking, we would use rods and reels to see what we could catch. It was a great summer job. I was sure glad it wasn't illegal to have this kind of fun as one was doing such an enjoyable, interesting job—and being paid to do it.

As it was with most biological surveys, this one was an eye opener for me. On our first picking of the net we had several longnose suckers (*Catostomus catostomus*). Those fish are common in the "South-48," but I had never seen a sucker since coming to Alaska. Joe told me that they were in every fresh water drainage in the state.

Other species common to freshwater lakes in that area that showed up in the nets were, arctic char (*Salvelinus alpinus linneaus*), burbot (*Lota lota*), northern pike (*Esox lucius linnaeus*), slimey sculpin (*Cottus cognatus*), arctic grayling (*Thymallus arcticus*), and several types of whitefish including round, broad, and humpback whitefish. Bering Sea cisco, and least cisco, were found in most of the larger lakes. Prior to this survey I'd been aware of only char, grayling, burbot and whitefish, along with some smaller, guppie-like finny critters.

We were surveying a minimum of four lakes per day until the weather turned sour and blocked our efforts. Rain and fog kept us in camp for two days. To beat the damp chill, we often sat in the BLM pick up, with the motor and heater running, telling our best jokes and stories, but we soon ran out of tales to tell. Being experienced travelers of the Alaska bush, Joe and I had several paperback novels to counter the boredom, but on the second afternoon of fog we drove to Nome for a restaurant meal, then took in a movie, appropriately *North to Alaska* was playing. Following the movie, we swallowed some beer and wallowed about as we danced with the local talent and tourists at the hotel bar.

The forecast was for more adverse weather, so after dinner and some brief dancing, we visited the Board of Trade Saloon. It was strictly historical interest that took us there, of course. That bar had been established by none other than

Wyatt Earp, after he left Tombstone, Arizona. It was pretty wild on weekends, but during the week, its clientele showed a palpably morose demeanor.

Hank, at eighteen, was still an underage minor, so as far as drinking was concerned, he could not join us in that emporium of sinners. Instead, Hank knocked about the town, seemingly entertained by the novelty of the old gold mining community.

By 2013, this same Hank was running a large gold mining barge that he had built himself. He and several other dredgers were featured on a reality television program called Bering Sea Gold.

Well, just before the last call, I was sitting at the bar over a glass of beer when a guy behind me, a complete stranger, shoved my head forward, causing me to cut my lip on the rim of the beer glass. My assailant had not uttered a word or given any warning before he struck me. I looked around and saw a fist coming my way. I was able to dodge enough to take the punch as a glancing blow and got one of my own off which connected with his nose. He just collapsed. I think he was drunk. The bartender called the cops. They took some statements after establishing that the guy was alive and was the perpetrator of the unprovoked assault on me, then the cops hauled him off to jail.

My right hand hurt. The drunken idiot just felt like slamming someone, it seemed, and I was a handy target.

It was time to go back to camp. The villain happened to be an Alaska Native and I am a blonde white guy. So did that have something to do with it? I didn't care. I just did what seemed natural. Hate crimes were not in the vocabulary yet and I think we need to look askance at such crimes today. It's simplest and best to just deal with the crime, rather than try to determine the motive.

Joe and I had only a few beers over a period of several hours, but we thought it prudent to let Hank drive. The rain and fog reduced visibility to just beyond the range of the headlights. A few miles out, the truck slid off the elevated roadway and stopped in a ditch, forcing us out into the rain and mud in our efforts to get the vehicle back on the road. We were successful both in getting the truck back on the road and in becoming well coated with mud, and thoroughly chilled. Hank turned the vehicle around and we went back to town, where we rented a room at the Polaris Hotel, took showers, then slept, warm, dry and comfortably.

The next morning came with no discernible improvement in the weather, and my right hand was painfully swollen, so we elected to spend that day in town, too. I wrapped my broken right hand in a Ace bandage and swallowed some aspirin. After the evening meal, rather than risk a repeat of the previous evening, we drove out to Salmon Lake, had a drink and crawled into our sleeping bags. At least we had been able to clean up.

Glacial Lake was on the list to check, but when I flew over it, I knew that I could safely land, but I was insecure about taking off safely, especially with a passenger, so I refused to put the Cub down. Eventually, several years later, Joe got to that lake via helicopter and found arctic char that apparently had been isolated for centuries, or millennia, and had evolved into several "niche types," each of which lived a unique life style in that isolated body of water. He wrote an interesting paper on the unique adaptation of the fish.

When it came time to head home, I tied some rails from one of the abandoned narrow gage railroads on the floats to use someway yet to be determined, sometime in the future. I looked forward to more such surveys with BLM.

The next summer the Bureau of Land Management decided to do some fish inventories in the Baird Mountains north of Kotzebue to see what species might inhabit the upper parts of the drainages. This work was done during late summer with water levels at their lowest. Only small dip nets would be required for this shallow water project, but fishing poles were used as we worked down our way downstream.

At the uppermost reaches of the streams, well past the last pools large enough to support small grayling we found slimy sculpin (*Cottus cognatus*) which apparently were able to subsist on insect larvae in the alpine streams hundreds of river miles from their normal littoral, or coastal, zone.

As one would expect, the further downstream we worked, the greater the number and size of fish and species we encountered.

Most of the streams are braided with a main channel appearing only intermittently in their course. We caught old, but small grayling (*Thymallus thymallus*) much further up the drainages than had previously been recorded.

One of the lakes on Seward Peninsula.

Some petrified coral heads found in the mountain streams.

Both arctic char *(Salvelinus alpinus)* and Dolly Varden *(Salvelinus malma)* were caught in increasing numbers as we progressed downstream.

Some of the mountain streams were littered, practically paved in places, with Paleozoic fossils, primarily those of corals, brachiopods and gastropods that formed during the Carboniferous and Permian periods.

In the previous years I had hunted through the areas near every place we surveyed, so the abundance of fossils was not a surprise to me, but the biologist was impressed.

The BLM Hydrologist

In July, 1979 I got a contract with the Bureau of Land Management to fly my Super Cub on floats—that was N7156Z—to Galbraith Lake, from whence I would be transporting a hydrologist to lakes in the area for the purpose of estimating water volume, chemistry and fish populations.

We were working primarily in the Arctic National Wildlife Refuge, commonly referred to as ANWR—pronounced "An-were."

After topped off all four of the eighteen gallon wing tanks, I loaded two cases of engine oil and belted them in the rear seat, along with my tent and other survival gear, before I left Kotzebue. My route of flight was easterly, up the Kobuk River, skirting the south slope of the Brooks Range. I flew by Walker Lake, and passed through hundreds of miles of wild country, enjoying the pristine scenery as I passed through.

Time was approaching for a urinary break, so I began to look for some interesting spot to land and perhaps linger for an hour or so. A small lake showed the outlines of stone age dwellings, caches, or rock structures of some sort, so that was more than enough to draw me in. Berries were beginning to ripen, fish were breaking the surface of the lake and ancient caribou trails indicated previous passage of great herds of the tundra deer. I wondered how many other men had been treated to the sights I was enjoying.

Daydreams of the daily life of those who had made shelter here in centuries past filled my imagination. The main business in ancient times had to have been scratching up enough food to sustain their little family group, but those who gathered and arranged the large boulders had enough time to construct this camp which was much more than just a temporary shelter. They must have been rich in comparison to most of the ancient nomads. In any event, they were certainly self sufficient, because they had

A prehistoric dwelling site.

to be. And, unlike so many of their time, they left obvious evidence of their occupancy and use of the land.

But I had a long way yet to go that day, so I ate a bite of lunch and reluctantly departed that very beautiful, private piece of paradise.

Iniakuk Lake and the Alatna River passed beneath my wings before I turned North, into country through which I had not traveled before.

How I loved this job! I felt like an explorer. And I was being paid to do this!

Following the John River through Anaktuvuk Pass, then finally turning easterly, crossing the Kanayut, Nariushuk and Itkillik Rivers before arriving at Galbraith Lake, some seven and a half flying hours later, it had been a very special day for me. The whole trip had been at less than three thousand feet elevation and most of the time I flew at less than fifteen hundred feet, as scattered rain and snow showers accompanied me the entire distance, making a direct route impossible. Yeah, I said rain and snow—in July.

We had no Global Positioning System (GPS) guidance apparatus available in those days, but the maps (aviation sectional charts) were accurate and my Cub, which had a double set of wing tanks, had a nine hour range when all tanks were full. I landed on Galbraith Lake with about fifteen gallons of fuel unused. For most of the flights from the base camp I would not need to be departing with a full fuel capacity, until it came time to head back to Kotzebue.

Galbraith Lake lies adjacent to the Trans Alaska Oil Pipeline. The Bureau of Land Management (BLM) had brought several trailers up the haul road and had set up a very nice camp with a heated cooking and dining hall, sleeping quarters and other trailers for the use of scientists, pilots, cooks and other camp workers. Two of the trailers were modified to serve as laboratories for field analytical work, sample preparation, and cataloging of data. This was the most comfortable camp from which I had ever been based. It sure beat the cold wall tents we used while doing a caribou survey on the north slope in March of 1977. We even had access to a warm shower in this luxurious camp. A laundry unit was available to allow us to keep our clothes clean.

Upon my daily return, I would advise the camp on the unicom frequency before landing on a small lake adjacent to Galbraith Lake. If a strong wind came up, as is common throughout Alaska, the large lake could produce waves large enough to sink or otherwise damage my small, fragile float plane. It was much safer and more sensible to leave the Cub overnight on the small lake.

When I had secured N5156Z with tie downs and gust locks, the camp's Bell Jet Ranger pilot would crank up his chopper and come to pick me up. We would then sling some barrels of aviation fuel and a pump to my moorage spot. The pilot had flown choppers in Viet Nam and was as devil-may-care as any man I had encountered. He remarked that, by my clothes, I must be an Alaskan, as locals dressed so plainly. He was especially well groomed and dressed quite nicely, compared to the rest of the crew and he seemed very happy all the time. His demeanor could be described as giddy. His perpetual hilarity set an alarm off in my head, but then, helicopter pilots are known to be crazier than most, so I left it at that.

The hydrologist was a most interesting fellow. He was truly a water specialist and loved his vocation. I heard more tales about water, its unique characteristics and nature than I had ever heard before or would hear again. But it was all interesting. Plus, he loved to fish at least as much as I did.

We rigged up a sonar device between the float (pontoon) spreader bars and had a line to the back seat where he set up a display and recording instrument. When a sizable fish appeared on the sonar, he would tell me to chop the power and we'd both rig up our fishing poles. Trolling or casting from the floats of the plane were equally productive. The fish in these waters had seldom, if ever been offered the choice of lures we threw to them. We landed a lot of lake trout, (*Salvelinus namaycush*) but none were as large as those I had caught in Feniak or Burial Lakes which are north of the Noatak River and only about forty miles from our lodge on Trail Creek. Most of the fish we caught in this area weighed three to five pounds.

The flesh of some of the lake trout was pale with a creamy white hue, but that of others had an orangish color. The different flesh tones were clearly visible on fish caught in the same locations. I had seen this in lake trout from other parts of Alaska, also. The few Lakers that I caught in the Noatak River all had white flesh, but fish from the nearby lakes might have either pale or orangish colored meat. So why the difference? It was suggested that the difference was likely attributable to the diet, but I assumed that fish from the same area must feed on the same prey. And I never did find an explanation for the dichotomy in color. Since that time, in 2014, I read an article that maintained that king salmon (*Oncorhynchus tshawytscha*) with white flesh (the oiliest and most delicious of all) had a genetic recessive trait that prevented them from metabolizing carotenoids found in their feed. This explanation might apply to the lake trout too, I assume.

I did notice that the Lake trout in these lakes had unusually pronounced, and noticeably protruding vents, or anuses. Their stomachs were filled with hard shelled snails, which perhaps explained their furunculated, cauliflowered anal sphincters.

My curiosity had years before led me to investigate lake trout. I learned that these forked tailed fish are a member of the "char" group of trout, which included arctic char, Dolly Varden and brook trout. Lake trout do not reach sexual maturity until they are five to eight years old and members of that species spawn every other year or even less frequently in northern Alaska. It is not uncommon to catch twenty year old fish and they are known to live up to fifty years. The females tend to be larger than the males.

Though excellent table fare, they do not taste as good as arctic char or king salmon, in my opinion.

We put in some pretty long days to expedite the project and at times encountered low ceilings or snow. The Alaska Offices of Aircraft Services had some unreasonable restrictions, considering the vagaries of weather,

A twenty pound lake trout from Feniak Lake.

cost of operations in remote locations, etc. I was always safety conscious, but due to extenuating weather circumstances, sometimes we found it necessary to fly a bit longer on a given day than the rules prescribed. When my time was totaled and turned in for payment, the Anchorage office docked me for a significant amount of time. My appeal was denied and I never did get paid for some of my flying time. Government can be all too arbitrary and its regulations are self defeating at times. But, we got the job done safely.

Passing through the mountains I saw many more Dall sheep (*Ovis dalli*) than similar habitat carried in the Western Brooks Range. We saw musk oxen (*Ovibos moschatus*), moose (*Alces gigas*), caribou (*Rangifer tarandus)*, grizzly bears (*Ursus arctos horribilis*) and wolves (*Canus lupus*) during the course of the project.

Dozens of species of birds were found in abundance. Small game and rodents were plentiful as well.

The hydrologist and I were impressed with the great beauty of this vast wilderness. However, we were also dismayed at some of the litter and careless lack of stewardship we encountered.

Elusive lake is truly a gem, but some guide had used it as a base camp for years and we found his plywood cabin in total disarray with an estimated five hundred old square, five gallon aviation fuel cans blown across the tundra for more than a mile in all directions. Such unconscionable littering

Elusive Lake in mid-July.

should be met with clean up and/or criminal charges, but most often they are just ignored. In fact, the worst instances of litter and degradation of wilderness I have seen were done by the federal government in Chittistone Pass in the Wrangel Mountains and in many places on the north and south slopes of the Brooks Range.

During World War II, the Federal government had explored for oil on the North Slope, leaving behind wooden derricks with supplies and equipment scattered about. Caterpillar operators had lowered their blades cutting the operator's initials or maybe those of his girl friend, and other marks into the tundra. The gouged tundra had since thawed out, leaving muddy quagmires in the otherwise pristine setting. Large dumps of fifty-five gallon fuel and oil barrels were scattered over numerous places in the remote far north.

A High of a Different Kind

One evening we walked into the dining hall a bit late, having been delayed by waiting out a dense snow storm that caught us miles from camp that July afternoon. Pizza was the main course and everyone seemed to be in an unusually good mood. Two lady scientists, neither of which I had seen to so much as crack a smile before, were laughing and carrying on like school girls. Being hungry, I loaded up my plate and ravished two large slices of the pizza provender. When I returned to get a slice of apple pie, everything seemed incredibly funny. The whole assemblage was laughing and I joined them.

I was sharing a sleeping trailer with the chopper pilot and had seen him toking hand rolled cigarettes and figured it must be marijuana. It dawned on me that the cooks must have laced the pizza with cannabis, which had induced the extreme hilarity in the entire company. I went to the kitchen and discreetly told the head cook that I knew what was going on and if she decided to try that again, to at least cook my meal without any mind altering drugs or I would see to it that the camp manager was informed of her "seasoning." I assured her that if she did it again I would pursue her and her actions to the fullest extent of my ability and be a credible witness for the prosecution after her arrest. I was angry and totally serious, in spite of the normally mellowing effects of the pot. The cook stopped giggling and seemed to take me seriously. And I did not fall victim to inadvertently consuming any loco weed again.

I'd never been interested in experimenting with any drugs. My life and days had always been full, with no room for such a waste of time and consciousness. I was concerned that the mellow state I felt that night might not be discernible, but still subtly influential, the next morning, when I needed to fly. But I flew without complications the following day.

As we entered the sleeping trailer, the chopper pilot invited the two cooks to join us. Those three celebrants tried their best to assuage my concerns. I told them that I was dead serious about future meals. With the real potential for more snow storms or other difficult weather, I wanted to be in full control of my facilities, as well as my aircraft. I could live with being thought of as a prude, with no problem.

This one was a freebie, but if it happened again I would raise Cain about it, I assured them.

I didn't mention this to anyone else and suppose that none of the rest realized what had happened. Most were probably like me,—virgins, to the use of the weed.

One afternoon as we were headed back toward Galbraith Lake, we again ran into some heavy snow squalls. The lakes were all open and there were plenty of good spots to land, so I steered toward a good looking body of water and when I touched down, I made out a mobile oil exploration camp on the far edge of the lake. I taxied close to the camp and we were treated to a fine hot meal and watched a taped movie until the weather improved.

In spite of frequent bouts of foul weather, we got more lakes surveyed and cataloged than the project manager had set as his goal. This was only possible by flying a bit more on some of the good days than the guidelines dictated. But we got 'er done!

As the BLM camp was being readied to close down for the season, I topped off my fuel tanks and headed back west for Kotzebue right after a hearty breakfast.

I always made it a point, whenever possible, to travel a different route from those I had previously followed. Even a mile or so from an often used course increased my familiarity and appreciation of the country. With more than twenty hours of daylight and a couple extra hours of fuel for the return trip, I sashayed through the Brooks range with some short side trips to check out places I'd not seen before. I was surprised to encounter stone structures on several of the lakes on the south side of the mountain passes. Some of the stone edifices were so small I surmised that they were likely used as meat caches, rather than shelters for people. Deep, old, caribou trails lead through the passes and it seemed likely to me that prehistoric hunters would wait for the animals to come, and if their hunting success was good, they could store surplus meat in the stone caches. It would follow that such stores would keep better if stocked with meat from the cold weather autumn migrations.

I landed on several lakes and toward the end of the day I caught a half dozen lake trout to take home.

The whole time I kept reminding myself how lucky I was to be able to access this wild country in its still relatively pristine state. I lamented that the wild country could not last this way forever.

Right Hand of GOD

The local Jesuit Priest, Father Mike Kinecki was one of my best friends. Though I was never a Catholic, I admired the work of this true Man of God and we enjoyed each other's company on hunting and fishing trips as well as over many dinners and glasses of wine, or whiskey at my home.

Kotzebue was served it's fair share of self frocked soul savers, most of whom seemed to think that the general public owed them plenty for sacrificing themselves to be present in that remote Arctic village, working to save the souls of others. Their perceived "due" often included free dental care. I did offer free tooth carpentry and mouth plumbing to Father Mike Kinecki and his staff, but not to most of the others, especially the "hellfire and brimstone" types, as well as others who assumed it was only right that they receive freebies due to their chosen line of work.

In September, 1980, Mike asked me if I had time to take one of his brother priests bear hunting. Father Mike told me that the padre he had in mind had been recruited from the congregation someplace down South after having worked as an electrical engineer. He heard his calling to the priesthood and was a fine member of the clergy, according to Mike, whose word was always good enough for me. I agreed to take him. This priest had savings from his previous life pursuits and intended to pay for his trip. That was a nice, though uncommon aspect of taking the friend of a friend hunting.

Earlier that September, my wife Mae and I had been watching a huge bull moose on the Nimiuktuk River, East of the lodge. This monster had bones on his head that spread over seventy inches and were beautifully formed. The only reasonable access to that great beast was to be gained by landing on a short, twisted gravel bar about a mile from the moose. If we could get the Cub on that strip, we could set up the tent and have a good chance of popping the bull in the morning. The bull was keeping a dozen cows or more in check and a gang like that is not apt to move too far overnight, unless they were seriously molested by bears, wolves or men. It would take at least four lightly laden trips in the Cub to get us with the meat and antlers off that little bar, but it would be well worth the extra effort for a rack like that, if I could land on the bar.

The nasty little strip was marginal. I set up, trimmed the plane, pulled down full flaps, and drug the Cub in on the margin just above stall speed. But when I touched the wheels to the surface, I could see that we would not get stopped before going over a cut bank and into the river. No animal is worth an airplane … or a wreck. I shoved in full throttle and we got out of there. That big moose was safe, for the time being.

The priest, Father Jim, was after a grizzly. By the time he arrived, the lakes and rivers were pretty solidly frozen, but little snow had fallen. We saw one big bruin sitting in a patch of snow he had scraped together on a western facing hillside. He was just sitting there on his hind end, apparently waiting to be drifted over by the next easterly wind and snow storm. He was a worthy prize, but more than eight miles of extra tough mountain walking separated him from the lodge, so he was safe where he sat.

After several days of hunting from the lodge with no opportunity arising for the priest to get a bear, I decided late one afternoon to have a look at the big moose that Mae and I had coveted. As I flew toward the spot I saw no cows. That was not a good sign. Then a big grizzly stood up in the brush. He was feeding on a kill, and a closer fly-over inspection revealed it to be that giant bull moose. This seemed to be a gift from heaven. Here was the big moose, at least the rack was available and possibly, in that cold weather, at least some of the meat. If the Padre killed the bear, I might be able to acquire part or some of our winter moose meat without firing a shot! I've never minded using fresh road kill, or predator killed meat. I've noticed that it all tastes the same once it's in the pot.

With the tent in the plane, I headed toward the nasty, crooked little gravel bar. It looked a bit more doable now, as the water level had dropped, exposing a bit more length of dry gravel on the downstream end.

And in addition, I figured I had God's own right hand in the back seat. That should trump any set of beads or good luck charms.

So, cautioning the Priest to brace himself on the overhead cross bar as the landing might turn out to be rougher than usual, I trimmed the Cub, dropped the flaps and committed to land. The main wheels touched gently just at the threshold, I dumped the flaps and stood on the heel brakes. But suddenly it became apparent to me that dirty little strip was still too short! I gave the engine full throttle and just at the end of the strip, on the lip of the cut bank, I jerked on full flaps. We lifted off, struggling over the stream, before the Cub began to settle. I gently eased the stick forward to lower the nose and avoid a stall. My main wheels struck the top edge of the cut bank on the opposite side of the river and the tail came up, but with my hand holding the throttle jammed full forward, the Cub staggered along, just over the tops of the pucker brush (dwarf birch bushes). We began to gain a little airspeed, but the Cub was still in a near stall situation.

I felt the back of my seat being bunched up in the clutching grip of the Priest, as he hung on for dear life. A lone skinny cottonwood tree was right in front of us and I didn't have the altitude or airspeed to turn away from it. The left wing hit the snag, snapping the tree off and slowing us down noticeably, but the Cub mushed along, and stayed in the air. Thank God!

Once we were out of the squeeze and had safe flying speed I said, "The Lord is with us today, Father!"

"He's always with us, my son," the Priest reminded me, before asking, "Are you going to try to land again?"

By then I had dumped the flaps, trimmed the Cub and was peering out the side window trying to see what damage the left wing had sustained.

"No, Father Jim, we are going to return to the lodge and survey the damage," I told him. The thirty minutes back to the camp seemed to pass slowly, due to my anxiety regarding the damage to the wing, but we made it without further incident.

Inspection at the lodge revealed that my landing and taxi light bulbs were broken, which I replaced, and then I went about strengthening the broken Plexiglas lens with heavy visqueen and duct tape.. We were so lucky that far worse had not befallen us. The Cub performed just fine as it was and I was able to replace the Plexiglas lens over the lights with a new piece back in Kotzebue later that season.

We spent the next day thankful for being spared an experience that would have been at least embarrassing, or at worst, possibly injurious, to one or both of us.

Additionally, the flight plan I had filed in town was to the lodge and return to Kotzebue in ten days, so a wreck thirty or more miles away would mean we would probably spend quite some time in that area before a search was initiated and a rescue plane could locate us.

The next day I decided that we should at least return to check on the great bear in hopes of finding a more suitable landing site. The temperatures were dropping and soon the smaller lakes might be usable, affording us such an opportunity.

So, light on gas and with a spartan tent camp in the back, I cranked up the Cub and we flew back to see if that great bear might be still feeding on the big moose. Indeed, he had not yet consumed his kill, but that gravel bar no longer held any attraction for me. I looked at a narrow lake within walking distance, but the ice looked a little too dark, so I decided to give it another day before touching the main wheels on it to see if it was safe to land on. We flew back to the comforts and warmth of the lodge.

After brunch the next day we set off again. We found a smaller grizzly rooting around the kill site but the big bear was not to be seen. I did test the lake ice by touching down and running a way to leave wheel prints, then pulled up and flew over the marks. No water was coming up in the tire tracks, so I reckoned the ice was thick enough to land on, but probably not strong enough to leave the plane sitting on any longer than absolutely necessary. So I landed along one edge and taxied up onto the gravel at the end closest to the bear kill.

We glassed a few caribou grazing as they slowly headed south. From our bags in the tent that night we heard a mournful wolf call, a long way off.

The first thing the next morning we had a cup of coffee from my thermos and a few cookies before striking off for the bear. We walked as fast and as quietly as we could to the site before setting up on a hill to scrutinize the area with binoculars. But we found no bruin. I decided to remove the moose head and take it with us. I told the Priest he could have it if he wished. The meat, what was left of it, was frozen brick hard. It would feed whatever carnivore found it, which most likely would be a wolverine.

The grizzly had killed, eaten and left.

N3421P

The rack was worth taking out.

As we walked back with the moose rack we encountered a smaller bull with three cows. The bull mounted a cow as I was filming. Both Father Jim and I were fascinated by the quick affair. Later I apologized to the Priest, asking if he thought he might be in trouble if the Pope heard that he had been present and assisted in filming pornography in the wild. He assured me that it would be okay and likely never known to anyone but the two of us.

The good Priest did not get his grizzly, but said he had thoroughly enjoyed his experience, which I was glad had not included being rescued or potentially much worse.

Back in Kotzebue, Mae made us one of her fantastic dinners and as she served it, the Priest said he would like to offer grace. He said I always remembered to do that, even up at camp.

Fact is, at some meals I had forgotten to offer thanks or ask the padre to do so.

He was a very gracious Priest.

Drop Out Problems

In September, 1986, I had a wonderful group of Germans at the lodge on Trail Creek. I had exchanged cooks, replacing a French woman from near Paris who did elegant, light meals, but she was not at all into the "meat and potatoes" type of high calorie requirements of the active group of German hunters.

I replaced Eliane with a recently widowed cousin from Iowa named Alice. That farm lady knew how to cook for a group of hard working men and she did some wonderful deserts and cookies as well. She was great in camp.

That year I had also hired a young local fellow named Tom, and helped him get licensed as an Assistant Guide. Tom told me that he did not mind chopping wood, fleshing capes and packing meat, but he would sure appreciate a chance to be out in a tent with a hunter. This young man was keen on guiding and I thought he held great promise for future efforts with me and eventually his own guide operation.

It had been my practice, when game locations and weather conditions warranted, to fly out with a single guest and my tenting gear We then hunted on foot from the temporary camp, leaving my Assistants and other guest hunters at the lodge to hunt from there.

If adverse weather developed, in one trip I could have the camp, guest hunter and myself airborne and back to the comforts and safety of the lodge, or town. Certainly my gross income would have been improved by dropping several Assistants out with one guest each, then returning to retrieve them after a few days. Having several satellite temporary camps out would be financially rewarding, but along with the positive financial aspects of such a system, I would be spending more of my time expediting others forth and back. And my liability exposure would be magnified. Most of the successful guides in Alaska did operate that way, but in my case, I was concerned that unforeseen problems might develop. Guest and staff safety were solely my responsibility, so in my attempt to minimize my liability, I just did not use drop camps for other than myself and a single guest. I opted for less money, less risk and more personal participation and satisfaction in the hunts. I'd much rather be guiding than flying.

"When it's working, don't fix it" is a good rule to follow, but I understood the young guide's point of view, as I had felt similar when I first began assistant guiding, so I mulled over the pros and cons, though the cons clearly tipped the balance to the negative. After reflecting on my own feelings from my time as an assistant, some twenty years before, I was leaning toward giving him his shot at more responsibility and something closer to independently guiding a hunter for a big animal. As things developed it was to be the largest of wild animals available to us ... a bull moose.

Tom was a hard worker and one evening as he was cutting wood for the sauna, he mentioned to me again, that he would really like to get out with a hunter or two. He said the lodge was great, but he was keen on being responsible for a tent operation.

I decided that I would make an exception for this fellow.

Moose were not as plentiful in the valley of the lodge that September, so one evening I took Tom in the Cub and located several big bull moose within a mile of a good landing spot on an alluvial fan just off Nunaviksak Creek, which was only about thirty minutes flight from the lodge. So I left Tom there to set up the tent and returned to the lodge for one of the Germans named Herman. I took Herman to the camp, dropped him and his gear off with Tom, and returned to the lodge, planning to pick them up in two days. With five world class bulls and about thirty other moose within a mile of the strip, I felt confident that the two men would have a big bull down early the next day. The ground was free of snow and conditions were ideal.

Herman was a young German forester with a great attitude and could easily pack a good load. He was an excellent woodsman—as good a guest as one could have, and an ideal person to put out with Tom on this endeavor.

As I departed the pair of hopeful hunters I told them I planned to return to check on them in two days, expecting them to bag a big bull the next day, following the mandatory overnight stay after being airborne. I allowed that they would spend the second day packing back the eight big loads of meat to the strip I had dropped them on, assuming weather and river levels remained as they were. By late on the second day, all or most of the meat and the rack should ready for me to load and take to the lodge. I would have to come back at least two more times for the men. If one more load needed to be packed in, Tom could do that as I flew out Herman with the second load.

The alluvial fan I chose for landing was the only suitable landing spot in the area. It ran northwest from its lower threshold and coursed uphill toward the mouth of a creek that came out of a steep gorge from the high mountains. The lay of the land dictated an uphill landing and a downhill take-off. The only approach and departure route would place the aircraft between two steep hillsides. However the departure route would be going down creek and toward lower terrane, which was advantageous.

That landing spot was smooth and plenty long at about a thousand feet, but it was uphill and once the pilot committed to land, a go-around was not possible due to the steep inclines at the upper end of the strip.

All things considered, it was a pretty decent bush strip.

The wind in that area usually blows gently down the strip, demanding a tail wind takeoff, but that negative aspect is overridden by the length of the strip and the downhill component, provided the wind is not too strong or gusty.

So weather the next day was nice and we had good hunting at the lodge, with our guests taking two caribou and a grizzly. Three wolves were seen, but none were shot. I expected that Tom and Herman had probably taken a huge bull moose.

Day two opened with a red sky. Usually a reddish dawn means a big wind is coming. "Red skies at morning—sailor take warning." That day an overcast moved in quickly from the south and by mid afternoon we were getting snow. The wind was out of the south at about twenty knots.

By the next morning we had over a foot of wet snow at the lodge, with scattered squalls in all quarters.

Things improved a bit in the afternoon. At five o'clock we got a break in the weather and I flew over to the drop camp to check on Tom and Herman.

A mere thirty minutes away to the West, conditions were vastly different. It had been raining hard in that valley and the creeks were all high. Some streams were already muddy. The wind was stronger in the narrow valley and it was blowing up the strip,- the opposite of what usually prevailed in that location.

When I flew over I felt significant turbulence, which coupled with a tail wind, would make any attempt at landing complicated ... and somewhat risky.

I was uncomfortable with the breeze, because for landing I would have to take it on the tail, but with landing upslope, I reasoned that would partially counter the effects of the wind. The turbulence convinced me to not make a steep turn in the tight valley necessary for landing downhill and into the wind.

The two men were waving to me from nearby the tent. I could see a pile of moose meat and a big rack at the lower end of the strip. It looked like they were ready for me.

I decided to give it a try, carrying more speed and elevation than normal due to the turbulence. And I resolved to land long in spite of the tail wind, counting on the up hill grade to allow me to get stopped before running off the end of the strip and into the gully through which the creek flowed.

I figured the take off should be relatively easy, being downhill and into the wind.

On final approach it seemed like I had it figured right, but as I approached the threshold a big gust of wind—a downdraft, or sinker—forced the Cub down onto the surface. Luckily, I had cleared the rough stuff down hill from the strip, but the plane hit the ground harder than I had ever experienced before ... or since. It seemed that the main tires came up even with my eyeballs when the plane impacted the ground. I kept the stick back and rolled out to a stop midway on the runway. Had I not been flying faster than normal on my approach, I probably would have been forced down short of the threshold, which would have been disastrous.

It was the roughest landing I had ever made. I was worried about structural damage to the Cub.

Tom and Herman came running to me. They told me that they were waving to warn me off and did not expect me to land, given the rough air.

I taxied to the tent at the upper end of the strip and immediately inspected the landing gear. Finding no damage, I took out my pocket knife and cut the fabric away from the gear clusters on both sides to scrutinize them more closely. No cracks or defects were visible.

Herman had killed a good bull moose. The head and antlers were at the camp along with most of the meat. I told Tom to get the rest of the meat as soon as he could, but that I would not be back until the wind laid down. I felt fortunate that I had not damaged the Cub and did not want to push my luck on that score.

I told Herman that I would take him and the moose rack out, along with some of the choice cuts of meat, but I would need to saw one horn off to reduce the drag from the antlers for what looked like was going to be a somewhat hairy takeoff. Herman agreed to the idea of sawing off one horn.

I sawed the antler with two offset cuts, then broke the remaining bone to allow reorientation later. Tying one antler on each side, rather than the entire rack on one wing strut, the load would produce negligible drag in what I though might be a bit of a white knuckle take-off. I loaded Herman's gear and the prime cuts of meat (tenderloins and back straps) into the Cub.

The temperature had dropped several degrees and snow was beginning to fall as we prepared to depart. The wind remained strong and gusty. I stood on each of the tires and did a careful inspection of the wings, assuring myself that no snow was sticking to the surfaces and no wrinkles appeared in the fabric which would indicate damage from the landing. I told Tom that I would be back for him as soon as conditions allowed and he waved us off.

I gave the already warm engine a full three minutes to warm up, double checked the aircraft trim, magnetos and carburetor heat, went through the full pre-take off CIGAR drill (Controls Instruments Gas Aircraft trim and Run up) held the brakes until I had full throttle and cut loose. As we ran downhill into the wind I kept the stick forward to run up on the main wheels and avoid coming off the ground until we had extra speed. Even with the large load we were airborne in less than three hundred feet. I dropped the nose to keep us about ten feet above ground level, hoping that a big sinker would not slam us back into the tundra, but we were gaining speed rapidly, and with the higher airspeed came safety. As we cleared the narrow valley I trimmed the plane for ascent.

I circled once to fly back over Tom. The Cub was severely buffeted by the wind, further convincing me that I was not coming back in such turbulence. Tom was waving to us as we disappeared around the canyon wall.

We returned to the lodge without incident.

After unloading, I once again carefully inspected the gear clusters, shocks and cabane "V," but found no sign of breakage or cracks. I looked over the wings and lower longerons, but found nothing amiss. That was a relief.

For two more days, as the blizzard raged, we sat in the lodge, enjoying Alice's cooking, with plenty of moose and caribou meat, extra cookies and other snacks to munch on as we watched the wind sock flutter and the snow get deeper. And we all commiserated with Tom, back at the windy, snowy strip in the tent. Needless to say, I was wishing I had not needed to leave him there alone.

On day five for Tom in the tent, the storm began to tire out and the weather seemed manageable, but, considering the snow on the runway at Trail Creek, I was pretty sure that I would not be able to land with wheels on the Nunaviksak strip. So I loaded a pair of trail snowshoes, an aluminum snow shovel, some fresh cookies and other food and three paperback novels. I put a note in the food package and flagged it with long strips of surveyors tape. My instructions were for Tom to tramp out at least six hundred feet of the upper end of the strip for me to land on. If he had time, a longer runway would be a good idea, reducing the possibility of us both having to spend time lengthening the strip when I was finally able to land. I told him that I would fly over on the first decent day and drop more food if necessary. Tom did not have a radio. Handheld radios were not common in those days and we had not yet heard of Satellite telephones.

We had about eight to ten inches of snow on the runway at Trail Creek which I drug smooth and packed down with the Honda three wheeler. Nunaviksak, I was soon to learn, had sixteen inches or more, with some much deeper cross drifts on the strip.

As I was warming up to go, my good German friend, Ulrich, suggested that he ride in the back to make the drops for me. That was a good idea, but on the chance that I might be able to land, I decided against it.

So, I got to the strip to find Tom waving, just as he had been when last I saw him! I made the first run and tossed out the food from about three

A lag bolt held the sawed off antler in place.

hundred feet. On the next pass I threw out the shovel. On my third run I dropped one of the snowshoes, but it snagged on the back seat belt and when I got it loose, it went out the open door prematurely and got caught between the horizontal stabilizer and the elevator. I was flying down slope with no obstructions ahead, but a jammed elevator is not a good situation. I jiggled the control stick forward and back and, after what seemed like half of forever, the snow shoe dropped free, landing in some heavy willow brush. I thanked God that it came loose. The surveyors' tape would make it easy for Tom to locate. On my next pass I launched the second snowshoe correctly and it landed near the tent.

The following day I made a trip to Kotzebue loaded with game meat and trophies and to get more groceries for the lodge. Horror stories of marooned hunters and flooded camps were making the rounds in town. The National Guard had been called to make helicopter rescues of some drop out hunters.

On my return to the lodge I flew by Tom. He had stamped out only about 300 feet for me to land on which was way too short considering the snow and drifts on the strip. I quickly scribbled a note, put it in an empty plastic bottle, tied on some surveyors tape and dropped it to him. My message was simple—NEED MORE THAN DOUBLE THAT TO LAND.

Two days later, Tom had prepared a marginal, but usable strip for me to land on with wheels. He said he was happy to get the cookies and food, but he told me that he felt a little depressed when he saw I had given him several novels. He figured all the reading material made it look like he might be there for longer than he preferred.

I'd noticed bear tracks around the area and Tom told me that a medium sized grizzly, that seemed to grow a whole lot bigger as darkness came on, had been hanging around. The bear was drawn, no doubt, by the smell of the moose meat that remained piled at the lower end of the strip as well as the smell on Tom's clothes. Strangely enough, the bear did not take any of the snow covered meat. I did not see the bear.

We worked a while on lengthening the runway, then we packed the meat close to the tent. When I returned I could quickly load the remainder of the meat from that one pile.

Our trip back to the lodge was uneventful, as was my trip back for the remainder of the meat.

Every year hunters get dropped out to hunt on their own by Air Taxi operators and Big Game Transporters. 1986 was no exception, and with the heavy snow, many had to be evacuated by National Guard helicopters.

In all, Tom spent a full week in my four man tent before I could land to pick him up. That was the first and last time I ever dropped an assistant out with a guest hunter.

The lesson for me was clear. I would go back to doing all the tent camps myself.

Nearly 23 years later, in early September, 2009 I was hunting out of the lodge on Trail Creek with some guests from Florida. The wind was from the northeast and snow was occasionally reducing the visibility to a quarter of a mile or less on Trail Creek. I mentioned that I was relieved that I had no need to do any flying that day. Later that week, when I got to Kotzebue I learned that a friend had been attempting to land at Nunaviksak Creek that windy, snowy day and had a bad wreck, totaling his Aeronca Sedan. I knew that he had experienced what happened to me, so long before, but the "sinker" downdraft had hit him well short of the threshold. Luckily he had sustained only minor personal injuries, and when we visited a week or so later, he confirmed to me that he had set up with a tail wind, but a down draft forced him to earth short of the threshold But for a few short seconds, that would have been my fate so many years before.

Local effects can have a huge influence on bush landings.

External Loads

Super cubs are amazing airplanes. They are light, relatively inexpensive to operate and to maintain, and they are very responsive to control pressures, even at reduced speeds. Many repairs and maintenance issues can be performed by a reasonably competent pilot. Those aspects, no doubt, are why Piper Super Cubs are, and have for decades been, the nearly universal choice of aircraft for Alaskan big game guides and others who frequent the Alaskan bush country.

When I began guiding, I had a Cessna 180. It was a 1959 model which I bought primarily for long cross country trips to perform dental services in rural Alaska. It was lighter and performed better than the later models. It came with hydraulic wheel skis which were invaluable for me, as I was flying during winter from frozen Kotzebue and Barrow to Valdez and Bristol Bay, where wheels were often required at any time of the year. The gear could be pumped to ski or wheel status in mid air or while on the ground. I used 650 tires with the skis and larger, size 850, tires for summer flights.

Having logged less than seventy hours when I purchased N5150E from Tony Bernhart of Kobuk, at first it was a lot for me to handle. It was really too much machine for anyone with so few hours as pilot in command, but I gained experience as I used it several times each month for the next five years without a wreck. Tony had taken good care of the machine, so did I, and the plane took good care of me.

As Five-Zero Echo was my only airplane, I used it for polar bear and other hunting. I "white knuckled" onto a tiny strip on the remote property we had selected for a homestead. The landing area had to be worked over before I could take off, so I had a wheelbarrow and tools in the back. I continued to use the Cessna 180 on that strip until I sold it five years later.

I squeezed that four seater aircraft in on some soft beaches, one of which held a seven foot wooly mammoth tusk that I felt I had to retrieve. (See the pictures in *Alaska Hunting: Earthworms to Elephants*) Some of the places I landed back then with that airplane I would not want to hazard with a similar aircraft today. Good as it was, the Cessna could not handily be burdened with external loads. And sometimes I needed to haul some long stuff.

So I yearned for a Super Cub. After three years of toenailing into tight places with the Cessna, and saving enough money, in 1973 I bought a Super Cub, N3421P, which as I write this in 2015, I still own and operate. I've owned three other Super Cubs, and flown dozens of others, but Two One Papa is the best flying airplane I have ever been privileged to fly.

Cubs are anything but comfortable on long trips. They are cold in winter and they are drafty and slow, always. But when I get into 21P, the machine feels like an extension of my own body, and that type of comfort trumps the cramped, drafty discomfort felt during the long, slow flights. The three other cubs I have owned and the dozens of others that I have flown are similar, but not quite so exceptional as 21P, my first one. That Cub, to me, is a bit like one's first kiss—memorable, unique, and never to be repeated.

Super cubs can carry external loads better than any other airplane that I am aware of. They are very forgiving, if rigged properly. I flew 21P from Anchorage to Kotzebue as I bought it, with no wing dihedral and the ailerons slightly drooped. It churned along at flap speed—less than eighty-five miles per hour when on cruise! When I got it home, I put in some dihedral and washed out the ailerons which resulted in only a slight decrease in its exceptionally good short field take-off performance, but provided a ninety-five mile per hour cruise speed. It was a good trade-off.

Moose and/or caribou racks can be tied securely on the wing struts of a Cub without risk or compromise to performance. Those same antlers can be hauled out on the float struts of a Cub. Lumber racks are available to rig underneath the fuselage for hauling long pieces of building materials.

When tying a rack of antlers to the wing struts of a Cub on wheels, one must pay careful attention to not damage the pitot/static tub under the left wing, or block the air flow over the horizontal stabilizer of the tail. Once my wife, Mae, shot an outstanding caribou that had huge double shovels

N3421P headed for town with caribou racks and meat.

of twenty-two inches in width. I tied the bigger set of antlers on the right wing struts and put a lesser rack on the left. When we took off from our lodge on Trail Creek, I noticed a slight buffeting. I checked the magnetos, carburetor heat, then the trim, but still the vibration remained. After flying about five miles without being able to establish smooth flight, I turned around and went back to my strip. I looked things over and racked my brain. I decided that those huge antler shovels were perhaps causing a disturbance in the air flow over the tail.

I pulled the big set of antlers off and set the rack a bit further outboard from the fuselage and tied it down again. When I took off, the flight was smooth. I never forgot that important lesson.

In the 1980s the Federal Aviation Administration, flying a desk from some place in Oklahoma City, decided that external loads were to be made illegal. Most guides had no other reasonable means of getting their guests' trophies out of the bush, so they continued as before. A few guides got pinched and fined by the FAA. It's pure lucky that I was not one of those. Thankfully, reason eventually prevailed and a special permit could be obtained which allowed those loads. I got a mechanic to check me out with a moose rack on each side, a caribou rack on each side and a mix of moose on one side and caribou on the other. It was time consuming removing and reloading the various racks, but it was well worth it all, if it kept me from an FAA violation. Of course the certified mechanic observed how

An extension ladder has no effect on Cub performance.

Loading onto float struts is easier.

Rolled counter top and a couple twelve foot 2X8s.

Moose rack on the wing struts.

little effect the head bones had on the aircraft's performance. I got the external load paperwork and permits. We gotta keep it legal.

When on floats, antlers can be secured to either the wing struts or to the float struts. Most times, I preferred to place heavy moose racks on the float struts, which requires much less lifting and awkward manipulating of the large, heavy set of antlers, and it keeps the center of gravity lower.

When building and maintaining the lodge which sits one hundred eighteen GPS miles north of Kotzebue, and is only accessible by small aircraft, one must make do with what's available. Lumber, ladders, rolls of counter topping, linoleum, etc, are sometimes needed at the camp, so I flew them up either inside or outside of the Cub.

Over the years I have hauled skis, replacement propellers for wrecked airplanes, extension ladders, lumber, posts, rolls of aircraft aluminum, gutted caribou carcasses, and many other things tied to the wing struts or float struts, with no problems.

Air Taxi Charters

The Piper Super Cub is a very specialized flying machine. A Cub flies much slower than most aircraft used for commercial hire. Cubs are cramped, drafty, and uncomfortable. They are cold in winter. And they normally carry only one passenger. Some cubs, like mine, are fitted with an extra seat belt to carry a second passenger, but the unfortunate soul who occupies the aft seat has zero visibility, and might envy the comfort of a canned sardine.

However, for low, slow flight with short take-off and landing requirements, nothing beats a Super Cub. For game and fish surveys the Super Cub has long been the air machine of choice.

Most of my air taxi charters involved government agencies doing fish or game surveys, but often I would take a trip for Shellabarger in his Cessna 180, or on rare occasions in a Cessna 206.

Summertime and the living is easy, or so the song goes. I stayed busy most of the year, but summers sometimes bordered on being frenetic. I serviced remote camps, dropped people off on rivers to enable them to float down stream and I did fish and game census surveys. Normally I picked the floaters up at an easily identifiable spot a week or so later. A few of the floaters made it all the way to the mouth of the Noatak, about six miles from Kotzebue where I picked them up, rather than having to brave the often turbulent water of Kotzebue Sound. Fewer still were those really stalwart adventurers who paddled all the way to town.

Biologist/Pilot

I came in late one July evening after a long day in my Cub on floats when Leon Shellabarger drove over to Poop Lake to tell me the latest news. He'd

On the upper Noatak River with some floaters from Japan.

knocked back a few Vodkas and was red faced and giggly when he pulled up. That afternoon he got a call from a federal agency back in Washington, D.C. They got word by radio that their biologist/pilot (whose name I will not divulge, but I will refer to him as RK) had run out of fuel on Seward Peninsula with their De Haviland Beaver on floats and the pilot was demanding that someone take him at least forty gallons of eighty octane aviation fuel immediately. Leon, who resented all tentacles of government, but none so much as the Federal arms, probably relished antagonizing this caller, as much as he enjoyed relating the story to me. My friend explained to the U.S. Fish and Wildlife Service man, that his float plane pilot (me) was out on another charter and would probably not return in time to make the fuel delivery that day. As there clearly was no emergency, Leon emphasized, he suggested the plane and passengers should anticipate spending some time that evening doing flight planning exercises in hopes of avoiding running shy of engine juice on subsequent ventures. Leon was giggling throughout his narration.

Leon said the official who called him was downright indignant that an emergency flight was not arranged to be sent out right then and there. The feds on the Beaver were not planning to spend the night with no accommodations or food and they were marooned amidst swarms of mosquitos, white socks, and other forms of flying pestilences.

Leon just gave him a ho-hum and suggested he call back in the morning. Obviously this surprise opportunity to bedevil a fed was the highlight of Leon's day.

Early the next morning I was having coffee and doughnuts with Leon at the hanger when the call came from Washington, D.C. Leon had decided that I should make the trip in my Cub as the Cessna was close to needing a hundred hour inspection.

Leon put the phone on speaker mode, to allow me to overhear the conversation. He explained that the fuel would have to be purchased and the round trip charter rate would have to be paid at the time of delivery of the fuel, or in advance. He wanted a federal purchase order number from the irate caller. After all, he explained, for all we knew, the guy on the other end of the phone was a phony, perhaps a crook or who knows what? Shellabarger carefully expressed those concerns to the unknown fed on the other end of the line.

The federal man screamed into the phone that no one should charge for rescue operations and people in rural Alaska should appreciate all the contracts they had been awarded by his agency, blah, blah, blah.

Leon told the guy that he should calm down before speaking with the seaplane pilot who was the only person available who could locate and assist the downed Beaver. I'm certain that Leon's muffled giggles were heard by the federal guy.

The federal bureaucrat's demeanor changed from one of demanding indignance to drippy sweetness. I told him what the fuel would cost and gave him my estimated flying time, which could be much greater if I had to search for the missing aircraft. I had the latitude and longitude coordinates given to Leon the day before, but nevertheless, a search could add to the flying time. I would not charge his agency for the first fifteen minutes on the ground, as his people poured the fuel into the Beaver, but I wanted the empty cans to take back to Kotzebue, as we would not allow anyone, even employees of the federal government, to litter our pristine wilderness. That was Shellabarger Flying Service company policy, I added.

Then I asked if the man was certain that the Beaver had a chamois and funnel aboard, if not, I would rent him the use of my own.

Of course the federal desk jockey had no idea about the availability of a funnel or chamois, he probably didn't even have a mental picture of what they looked like, so I sighed and said I would take mine along, just in case.

Leon was enjoying the conversation. He especially liked the bit regarding renting the funnel and chamois. "Nice touch, Jake," he congratulated me on that and lamented that he had not thought of it first.

Shellabarger and I thought alike on most issues, which explained our friendship, no doubt. We both reacted negatively to any semblance of bullying and were particularly vexed by pomposity and overly self-important people. The federal guy was a contender for top spot on our least desirable list—at least for the moment.

The day was clear with unlimited visibility, as had been forecast. The wind was light and variable. Upon lifting off from Poop Lake I headed directly toward the spot where the Beaver supposedly was sitting ... or, hopefully, floating.

When I arrived at the designated lake, there was no aircraft in sight. I circled over the body of water as I ascended to gain altitude to give me better visibility at greater distance. I sighted the federal Beaver about three and a half miles away on another lake, so I flew over to the site and landed.

The pilot, RK, waded out knee deep to catch the bows of my floats, but I waved him away. He really did not need to assist me and should have known enough to stay clear. I viewed his inappropriate action as an attempt to appear important, or maybe even knowledgable, to his stranded passengers.

The three passengers—two younger women and a man—all looked absolutely miserable. Their faces were sunburned and bug-bit which I could detect even through the head nets they wore. They did not have a tent or any sleeping bags available, so all had spent the night sitting on the lake shore, swatting bugs and being hungry. After giving his coordinates the pilot, RK, had flown to the other lake for some reason known only to himself. If the weather had been foul, locating the Beaver would have been complicated by that move. For all to hear, I mentioned the discrepancy in his reported location and where he now sat, but he ignored my comments.

When the eight cans were emptied into the Beaver, I retrieved the empty containers and my funnel before suggesting that RK follow me directly to

Kotzebue. The De Haviland beaver burned about twenty-five gallons of fuel per hour, so he had enough fuel to get to town with some to spare, but not enough to dilly dally around on the trip.

RK handed me his government business card which noted in bold script that he was a Biologist/Pilot as he assured me that he could get to Kotzebue on his own.

The Beaver's airspeed was about the same as that of my Super Cub, so I reminded him of that and that he needed to stop by Shellabarger's to sign the paperwork for the charter, gasoline and funnel rental. RK seemed shocked that the "rescue" was going to have to be paid for. I assured him that such self induced errors always cost the perpetrator and in this case, the person responsible was getting off cheap. The three passengers were obviously disgruntled at the unplanned overnight experience and remained silent for the entire conversation. But their glaring stares were boring holes into RK's back.

When RK got to Shellabarger's hanger he asked again if he really had to pay for the rescue. His three passengers accompanied him. Leon told him that his neglect did not constitute an emergency and our service was not a rescue, it was more like the bail out of an overly self important idiot. Leon's reply ended the discussion.

The federal agency withheld payment for the charter, gasoline, and funnel rental for sixty days, the maximum allowed, but finally it came, paid in full.

Imuruk Lake

One windy afternoon Leon called me at home. I had an anesthetized dental patient in the chair, ready to do some minor oral surgery. Leon said that a group of four federal people were at Imuruk Lake on Seward Peninsula. One of the group was ill and needed to be evacuated as soon as possible. The best bet was to take the Cessna 180 on floats, as he knew of no decent spot for a wheel plane to land near the place the group said they were located. I could use the Cub, but the Cessna was faster and could carry up to three passengers if necessary.

I told Leon that I could be ready to go in less than an hour, so he said that would do. He also suggested that I not rush through my dental procedure. Leon hated needles and all forms of dental or medical treatment and didn't want to further stress any person cursed with the need of a dental appointment. Leon was thoughtful that way.

Imuruk Lake was about an hour and a quarter direct run, one way, from Kotzebue. We had a solid overcast at approximately four thousand six hundred feet. The wind was blowing just a bit off the center of Poop Lake at thirty with gusts to forty-two miles per hour in town. With the stiff headwind, the trip might take twenty or thirty minutes longer. The take-off would be quick and easy, but I wondered about the water conditions at the lake.

Kotzebue Sound was solid white caps with swells up to four or five feet in height. Should I have to put the plane down in those conditions, I would likely damage or collapse the float struts and quickly capsize the plane, but since it sounded like someone was in real trouble, I flew directly across the Sound at four thousand feet on a 170 degree heading for the mouth of the Inmachuk River.

I flew over Cloud Lake and wished the party was there, as it was a smaller lake and did not look too rough to land on.

When I arrived at Imuruk Lake the group of four people was standing right where they were reported to be, but the swells were coming straight into the beach and were much too large for the plane to handle safely. Less than a half mile away was a small spit which broke up the swells and provided a much better and far safer landing area on its lee side. Why the people on the ground could not have figured that out and moved to the calmer water was beyond my understanding. But they weren't pilots.

I flew over the frantically waving group, wagged my wings and flew to the better landing area, then repeated the maneuver two more times. Apparently the folks understood my message and began to walk toward the better area. I noticed that all four were walking normally and carrying small back packs. But they left a large pile of gear on the beach. I landed, dropped the flaps and sailed backward to the beach where I set the heels of the floats on the gravel and waited.

The group arrived at the plane in less than thirty minutes, but the wind had picked up and the swells in the new location were building. We needed to load the invalid and get out of there as quickly as possible. I noticed no difference in the mobility of any of the group, so I wondered which one was sick.

The fellow who was reportedly suffering from severe abdominal pain was a hefty one. I estimated his weight at close to two hundred eighty pounds. He confirmed my guess, but with clothes and boots on, he weighed over three hundred pounds. I would have to taxi to the end of the small stretch of calmer water and firewall the throttle, but the end of my projected water run would put me into the big swells. I decided to begin my run with a downwind component, make a step turn to the left, and enter the big water with a right crosswind. That would allow me to make the last of my run, hopefully, in between a set of swells. I was tense and knew it would be a tricky departure. Timing of the swells would be critical, and luck more than anything else would determine whether I timed it to enter between the swells or not.

The other members of the group wanted to ride along. I told them that I could not take more than three passengers under normal conditions and in the situation at hand, even the guy I had was too much weight. The others were not happy with my reply and asked if even one of them could get a ride to town. I explained again that I was overloaded for the rough water already, but I would try to return if and when the wind and swells laid down, which would probably not be until the afternoon of the next day. I also instructed them to pack their gear to the protected beach behind the spit. They didn't like that idea at all! I figured they had about three hundred pounds of stuff in the pile they left on the other beach. Not much really, for a group that size. The three passengers and their gear would require two more trips, not just one, even in calmer conditions.

The departure was of the "white knuckle" variety, and would have been so much simpler and safer if my passenger was not double the size of a normal human being. I got the Cessna on step and reduced the throttle to less than full for the step turn. As I was straightening out from the turn I fire walled it. Before we came to the big swells I steered a bit to the right and was able to enter a trough between crests of the swells. When we rose to the top of the swell I pulled full flaps and we staggered off with the stall warning screaming. I held the nose high enough to avoid the tops of the oncoming swells. The plane hung on the prop for what seemed like half of forever before I could lower the nose and gain airspeed more rapidly. Man, I was glad to be out of there!

With the stiff tail wind we made it back to Poop Lake in an hour and two minutes. The passenger questioned me about the safety of crossing the

Sound at such a low altitude. I told him that I had come to pick him up via the same route and now we needed to get him to the hospital as soon as possible. My impression of the guy was that he was whiney and scared, and probably not all that ill.

In town I landed, secured the plane and told the guy to get in my pickup. He said he wanted to stop at the store to get some Pepsi before going to the hospital. Now, THAT made me angry. I drove him directly to the hospital and remained until I was told by the physician that he was okay. Apparently he had a bout of mild indigestion and gas, which I noted in the close confines of the plane—nothing more serious than that!

"So, you only had a tummy ache?" I asked the bloated human life form.

He said that gall bladder problems ran in his family and he was afraid that he was having an attack. I told him that the best therapy for gall bladder problems was walking, and I left him at the door. I doubt this fellow would have called for an emergency flight if he, rather than the American taxpayers were paying the bill. I was disgusted!

The next afternoon I picked up the other three people, hauled them to town and went back for their gear. I surmised from their talk that they had become worn out with their project, the isolation, and the relentless mosquitos, and decided to abort the mission. The alleged tummy ache was pure baloney, it seemed to me.

Service Man Gone Wacko

On a Saturday in March in the late 1970's I was having coffee at the hanger with Leon Shellabarger. It was a quiet day and things had been more routine than usual in Kotzebue for a month or more. It seemed almost dull. A brass plaque in the office proclaimed that "IN THIS LOCATION ON AUGUST 15, 1967—ABSOLUTELY NOTHING HAPPENED ". Life threatened to become downright pedestrian in our little remote part of the world.

Murphy must have read my mind. A call came in from Anchorage that an emergency charter should be dispatched as soon as possible for Cape Lisburne. The "dew line" commander at that location had called Elmendorf Air Force base in Anchorage and reported that one of the enlisted men had gone bananas and had become dangerously uncontrollable. He needed immediate evacuation to Kotzebue where he could be sedated and soon thereafter flown to the big military hospital at Elmendorf.

One Cessna 206 remained available at Shellabarger Flying Service, but his two pilots that were in town were both down with flu-like symptoms. It would be more than two hours before any of the chartered aircraft would return, according to their flight plans.

Leon mulled the situation over, lit up a cigarette and said, "Jake, you feel like making the trip? It would probably be best that you do it, as with your doctor training and all. That might come in handy."

"Hey, Leon, I'm a dentist, not a REAL doctor," I protested. I'd taken my check ride eight months before in a 206, but I had little time in that aircraft type. I was not keen on escorting a bushed-out whacko, either.

The weather at Lisburne was reported to be overcast with a six hundred foot ceiling, visibility was two miles in blowing snow, and a northeast wind at twenty-two, gusting to thirty miles per hour. Those were very doable conditions, considering that hostile location was often totally obscured in fog or snow with storm force winds.

As Leon and I evaluated the situation, one of the flu-afflicted pilots named Pete, came in. He was feeling better and was hungry for some flying time.

So the plan was for me to go home, get some emergency supplies, my sleeping bag, a thermos of coffee, and a couple of sandwiches. I would go to Lisburne with the Cessna 206 and Pete, the ailing pilot, as my copilot.

With the head wind component, we progressed a bit slower than anticipated, but were able to maintain an altitude of a bit over four thousand feet for the first seventy percent of the distance. We flew up the coast to Cape Seppings where the overcast forced us to reduce altitude and fly in visual contact with the snow covered ground.

Clouds shrouded the hills on our starboard side and the barely discernible shoreline faded into the nebulous blah of frozen sea ice on our port. But we had enough forward visibility to continue without intolerable stress. We got around Cape Thompson and steered west of the foothills. We noticed the weathered stands of rocks, which gave one the impression of sentinels standing on the slopes to the right of our flight path. My relatives and friends in Point Hope told me those rocks were called "stone men."

That name certainly augmented their spooky mystique.

The runway was constructed just inland from the beach and ran parallel to the shore. The easterly threshold was within easy walking distance of the main camp. With the wind coming almost directly down the runway, we flew over, banked left over the frozen ocean and set up for a final approach. The snow was blown free of the runway and the personnel had placed a dozen orange flags, clearly marking both sides of the strip. I touched the main wheels down and kept the yoke back until, as the aircraft slowed, I could no longer hold the nose wheel off the ground. We rolled to a stop in the section of apron used for transit aircraft and were met immediately by a four wheel drive vehicle, the driver of which invited us in for coffee and lunch.

The lunch was as large and tasty a steak sandwich as I have ever eaten. At least the inhabitants of this dismal site had a fine bull cook to help them forget the miserable weather and near total isolation during their year long assignment.

Then the senior officer, a uniformed U.S. Air Force Captain suggested we meet the passenger, who was currently a prisoner, and had been in supervised lock down for nearly twenty-four hours. The guy had gone off his nut the day before and was clearly a threat, primarily to himself, but to others as well. Through the small, heavy plate glass window in the door I could see the man was asleep in a recliner chair, trussed up in a straight jacket, and sleeping with his chin resting on his chest.

When the door was gently opened the restrained man, named Ernest, snapped to attention and struggled to free himself of the special garment he wore, but fortunately, his efforts were not successful. His entire body was boiling with angry energy which was, much to our relief, frustrated by the straight jacket. The sight of him gave me the feeling of a volcano about to erupt. The guy's roaring wails added to my consternation. This guy was a bruiser of a man. He weighed over two hundred fifty pounds and was not sloppy fat. If he got loose and took the notion to raise havoc he would be a handful for four strong men to control, especially in the confines of a small aircraft. His eyes were wide, with pupils dilated and he glanced around the room with a wild, but somehow vacant stare. He was a picture of pure, unfocused malevolence.

Restrained or not, I told the Captain that in view of the extremely violent nature and obvious strength of the man, I wanted to take two of his sober, responsible, strong men with us to escort the nutcase to the hospital in Kotzebue. If somehow, the berserk fellow got loose during the flight, he could seriously jeopardize the safety of all aboard, as well as Leon's airplane.

The Captain said he could not spare two more men, as he was already short handed, but I insisted on taking two helpers, and told him I absolutely would not allow the jacketed fellow to be loaded into the airplane unless my request was met. It was a charter flight and the additional passengers would not cost the government any more money.

We turned and walked back to the mess room. After twenty minutes, the Captain entered with two husky young fellows in their mid twenties who would make the trip with us.

The small base had an exchange store to which we were admitted. I bought a few small items—insulated coffee cups for my wife and me and a pair of shorts to use for racket ball. Pete grabbed up some porno magazines, which were not available in Kotzebue, along with a few other inexpensive things. The cook presented each of us with a hefty bag of food items, including steak sandwiches, candy bars and cans of Pepsi.

The Captain and company were obviously happy to be relieved of the unwelcome burden of the crazy man. Ernest had been at the site for less than two full months. In spite of the weekly infusion of movies, magazines and fresh, high quality food, some people are not able to handle the relative isolation of remote sites. Ernest was one such person.

With five of us in the Cessna for the return leg, and three of them heavier than average, we were close to our load limit, but the runway was nearly perfectly in line with the wind. I anticipated a routine low level route back to Kotzebue, but I did not load all the personal gear of the restrained man. The three hundred pounds of his gear that I rejected could go to town on the next mail plane.

We back taxied to the opposite end of the runway, I kept the plane on the ground until we had extra speed before allowing it to lift off. Then I brought the yoke back gently. We were airborne and headed for home.

We buzzed along at normal cruise speed below the overcast which initially was about two hundred feet above the surface. Low level clouds and moderate turbulence on the west side of Cape Thompson convinced me to fly

Cape Lisburne Is Often Obscured In Fog.

about three miles offshore over some rough pack ice where the air was smoother. GPS was not in use at that time, but the plane was equipped with an ADF (automatic direction finder) which began to pick up the Kotzebue NDB (non-directional beacon) about twenty miles south of the cape.

The conditions had deteriorated somewhat, but we had decent VFR (visual flight rules) with more than a mile visibility beneath the overcast which gradually lifted to six hundred feet by the time we were near Kivalina. I remained just off the coast to Cape Krusenstern, then traced our way to Sheshaulik and finally across Kotzebue Sound to the airport. I used the dirt runway 35 to land and we taxied to Shellabargers where an ambulance sat waiting for our "patient."

Still in the straight jacket with an Air Force parka on top, Ernest, by then in a calmer state, was taken to the Public Health Service native hospital where a physician sedated him and asked the two men from Cape Lisburne to accompany Ernest to Anchorage on the evening Wien Air Alaska jet. From there, Ernest was taken to Elmendorf Air Force Base hospital.

When the Cessna 206 was tied up and re-fueled, Shellabarger came out, slapped me on the back and asked how much I enjoyed normal air taxi work. I told him that I planned to stick with the Cessna 180 or my Super Cubs and focus on biological charters.

Aircraft Incidents and Accidents

Soon after I arrived in Alaska in June, 1967, I realized that an aircraft here was as important as a pickup or jeep in the South-48. When I became aware of the high cost of aircraft, I told myself that I would likely not own one, but I might have a pickup and a couple of boats. But in less than a year I was co-owner of an airplane.

With a bit over ten thousand hours of bush flying in the past forty-eight plus, years, I've been involved in a few mishaps and heard of others. I'll recount some of the more interesting ones here.

In February, 1968 I had flown in a Wien Air Alaska F-27 to Iliamna. From there I was to make dental field visits to native villages in the area, all of which but the nearest one, Newhalen, required traveling by small, single engine bush planes. I met Lonnie Alsworth at the lodge in Iliamna and learned that he was flying a Cessna 180 for a local air taxi operator. I liked Lonnie immediately and told him that I would ask for him to do the flying each time my assistant and I, along with our dental field gear were moved. He was an excellent pilot, in fact I would call him a "flyer,"—a term I reserve for the most exceptionally competent manipulators of flying machines.

Aircraft Accident

Defined as an occurrence associated with the operation of an aircraft taking place between the time any person boards the plane with intention of flight and all persons have deplaned, in which any person suffers death or serious injury or in which the aircraft sustains substantial damage.

Incident

Defined as an occurrence other than an accident.

We had completed our dental trips to Igiugig, Kokhonok, and Pedro Bay and had only Nondalton left to visit on the schedule. Lonnie flew in to pick us up for the last move, but that day he was flying a Piper Tri-Pacer on skis. The Cessna was out of service temporarily, so he was using his own little plane, which had less payload and performance capability than the 180, but it was all that was available at the time. He said moving us and our gear would take two trips in that plane, so my assistant and I, and part of our dental gear loaded in and we took off.

First Wreck

The villagers had used their snow machines to pack down the snow in front of the shore line on the frozen lake for use as a ski strip, but the job had been done hastily and large snow berms were left in the main landing area. A hard freeze the night before had solidified the berms, making them hazardous, but we came in and needed to land. Lonnie evaluated the situation, making two low level passes and decided that he could manage the conditions by holding back on the yoke to keep the nose ski from contacting the surface as long as possible. He gently touched down with the main skis and things were looking good until we contacted a berm at just enough speed to throw the plane into the air. When we hit the surface again it was right on top of another berm. This time the nose ski slammed down hard and collapsed, which brought us hard against our seat harnesses and to an abrupt stop. It was my first "plane wreck," but could accurately be called an incident, rather than an accident.

We removed ourselves and our gear from the plane and got to the school to set up the dental shop, while Lonnie went to a house with a HF radio and called his Dad, Babe Alsworth, who was a few miles away at Port Alsworth. Lonnie gave details of the damage and spare parts needed to put the Piper back into service.

Within three hours, the Tri-Pacer was again flying and Lonnie delivered the rest of our equipment to us before dark.

The Stinson

Lonnie and I became great friends and soon co-owned a Stinson 105 Voyager until we could afford a better machine. We planned to pay for the thousand dollar (I put up six hundred dollars and Lonnie added four hundred to make the purchase) airplane by hunting wolves, along with some beaver snaring and pursuits for other fur bearers.

In between periods of chopping firewood, Babe Alsworth gave me unofficial, but superbly practical flying lessons in his Taylor Craft and Piper Super Cruiser airplanes. Knowing that I planned to eventually make dental trips to remote villages and small towns that had no resident dentist, he advised me to purchase an aircraft with plenty of power and brakes and learn to use both properly. He also told me that "if you fly 'em, you're gonna wreck 'em," so be careful, but when it happens, don't let it beat you. Just climb right back in as soon as you can and go fly some more.

The Cessna 180

In 1970 I purchased a 1959 model Cessna 180 from Tony Bernhardt, of Kobuk, Alaska and flew it all around Alaska (except the Southeast Panhandle areas) without an accident. I sold it in 1975. Several times the horsepower was all that kept me from having serious accidents. Babe was right—get all the power and brakes you can, and learn to use them appropriately.

I tried to really pay attention to the flying. I made plenty of mistakes, but I tried to learn from them, and most of all, I tried to at least not make the same mistake more than once.

I made far more "off airport" landings than I did on approved runways. Wind velocity and direction are of paramount importance, and landing into the wind is clearly preferable, but under some circumstances it is not the best choice.

The amount of cross wind component must be gauged as accurately as possible before any unmarked runway, especially river bars, side hills, or ridge tops can be seriously contemplated.

The Cessna was wonderful, it cruised at 130 mph and I could carry three passengers as well as a fair amount of bulky, weighty gear, but the cost of maintenance was increasing, liability insurance was going through the roof, and I never carried hull insurance, which was even more expensive. I had made my field dental gear more efficient and less weighty and did not take an assistant with me as I hired a local gal in each place I served, so I could do it all with a smaller plane. Plus a Super Cub would allow me to comfortably squeeze into a lot of places that beckoned, but had not yet been visited by me.

The First Super Cub

In 1973 I began looking for a Super Cub. Wolf hunting from airplanes was still legal and my friend, Leon Shellabarger had mentioned that he would be willing to lease my plane, if I would fly it for him on his air taxi. A Super Cub was preferred for big game surveys, and the Alaska Department of Fish and Game needed a survey pilot/biologist in Kotzebue, so that Piper model seemed the ideal aircraft for me.

After months of looking in Trade-A-Plane and watching the Anchorage and Fairbanks newspapers, my guide friend and mentor, Jim Cann, called from Anchorage.

Jim told me that he'd found a 1958 Super Cub that looked pretty good—asking price was ten thousand, five hundred dollars,—same as I'd paid for the Cessna 180 three years earlier. I decided to go down to Anchorage to take a look at it.

Jim was a good mechanic as well as an accomplished bush pilot and he knew cubs. He flew it with me in the back seat. It's log books checked out and I bought it. Then he checked me out in it, accelerating my adaptation to this new, high performance, short take-off and landing (STOL) machine.

What a delight to fly it was! That little airplane felt like an extension of my body. It was cramped and cold compared to the Cessna and initially only cruised about eighty-five mph, but re-rigging it, by putting in some wing dihedral and washing out the drooped flaps brought it's cruise speed up to about ninety-five, which is a bit above average for a Cub. The previous owner had a Cal Center Stol kit installed with a cuffed leading edge, stall fences, and flaps extended all the way to the fuselage. It was, and still is, the best performing Super Cub that I have ever flown. I've owned others in the meantime, but I still have that Cub after over forty-two years of extensive, annual use.

I continued to fly the Cessna for long trips and for hauling big loads to the cabin, but I opted to use the Cub for most trips. I was logging about five hundred hours per year by then, double what I'd done when I owned just the Cessna.

Shellabarger was a man of his word and I leased the Cub to him, with the stipulation that I be the only pilot. He had several young pilots, but they were trained in tricycle gear aircraft. They were great with his Cessna 206s, but the young hotshot pilots wanted to use the Cub. I didn't want to be plagued with wondering what those cowboys might have put my plane through. Confidence in your machine is important. So, no one but me was authorized to fly my Super Cub on Shellabarger Flying Service. And I never loaned it to anyone under any circumstances.

Nosed Up On A Gravel Bar

It seemed like I could land anywhere. One beautiful summer day in 1975, after completing a week long caribou and raptor survey for the Alaska Department of Fish and Game, Mae, our labrador Zeke, and I took a trip north looking for washed up walrus, shed moose antlers or whatever else we might find. The Cub still had only the standard fuel tanks, with eighteen gallons of eighty octane gas in each wing, so I took along a few five gallon cans of extra gas, and a chamois filter. I intended to make a long day of it.

That day I'd landed on sand and gravel bars, on beaches with steep slopes, on ridge tops, alluvial fans, and other potentially hazardous places, all day long. I was feeling like I could land that Cub anyplace and take off, without worry. It was late in the evening as we headed back for Kotzebue when I flew over a small island in the Kuguroruk River and spotted a matched set of shed moose antlers. They were only medium size, but appeared to be intact and not sun bleached. They looked like they were in perfect condition. They would make a final addition to those we'd already stacked in the back of the cabin, and eventually they would be carved into something nice.

My confidence soared beyond my competence.

Conventional wisdom held that at about five hundred hours of bush flying without an accident, one tends to get over confident which inevitably leads to the first wreck. I had over 1,000 hours when it hit me.

A light wind was coming down the valley, the bar had a serious curve to the right, but overall I assessed the situation as a pretty routine bush landing. The rocks, all polished cobbles, were no larger than softballs and the middle of the bar was composed of primarily sand and pea gravel, ... or so it appeared to me as I flew slowly over it.

After flying over the spot twice at slow speed with full flaps, I nonchalantly set up for a full stop landing. I touched down just past the water at the lower end of the bar and dumped the flaps, holding full back on the stick. Before the tail wheel touched the surface, the Cub began to nose up. I had the stick in my belly and still the tail was coming up as the roll-out progressed. The middle area of the bar was way too soft and the big, soft, donut tires broke through a bit of a crust and our rate of forward speed suddenly diminished. As the nose of the airplane rotated toward the ground I was yelling, "No, No," but it was to no avail. If I had given it full throttle we would have not had enough space to get airborne before going into the river. We stopped with the propeller grinding into the gravel. The empty gas cans, moose antlers, sand from the floor, and the dog pitched forward in the cabin. I popped open the clam shell door and got out, the dog jumped out with me and I helped Mae onto the ground.

I felt lucky that the Cub had not gone all the way over onto its back. The main tires and propeller spinner were in three point contact with the ground.

How I wish I had a photograph of that, but I did not think to make one at the time, and I hope I never get another chance to record such a picture.

We were about one hundred miles north of Kotzebue which was well out of range for my radio. Weather was good, we had a tent and emergency supplies with us, but the first thing I wanted to do was to get the plane back in the three point position, lest it go on over and sustain severe damage.

I decided we'd better act soon, but remembered that I'd been told that often recovery efforts cause more damage than the wreck itself. I paused to think. If I lifted the nose and the tail came down too hard, the lower longerons would likely be bent, necessitating very costly repairs including welding and new fabric, as well as potentially preventing me from flying it out. I had to somehow keep it from slamming down too hard.

I removed everything from the cabin—tools, ax, shovel, tent, sleeping bags, empty gas cans … everything.

Mae suggested that as I lifted the nose, she could stabilize the fuselage and work her way toward the tail as it came down. This seemed our best bet, so we discussed it and began. That Cub weighed a bit less than 950 pounds empty, and it had only about sixty pounds of fuel left, some of

Not what I had intended.

which was beginning to dribble out. Clearly time was of the essence.

I lifted on the base of the propeller with one hand on each side of the spinner and immediately felt the center of gravity begin to shift toward the tail. As the tail came down, I hung onto the prop, hoping that my weight on that end would act as a counter balance to cushion the downward motion of the tail. Mae was scuttling along supporting the fuselage with her arms extended. Just before the tail touched the earth, the propeller turned a little and my right hand became wedged between the prop and the nose cowling. But the plane came down without much of a bump and without hitting Mae, who brought two of the empty gas cans for me to stand on as I extracted myself from the nose cowling of the aircraft.

I quickly inspected the longerons, which seemed to be none the worse for the experience. The prop had ground through a couple of revolutions before the engine quit and had pretty significant "gravel rash" on both blades, but it wasn't too severely bent.

I chopped down a medium sized spruce tree and had Mae hold it against the back of the prop while I used the blunt end of the ax to peen the prop nearly straight. I hacksawed off the terminal three inches of each blade which were badly chewed up—taking care to remove the same amount on each side. I filed it smooth and set a gas can under it to show where each blade passed, as I hand turned it through several cycles. The blades tracked reasonably true and I figured it should be okay to get us home.

I looked over the bar and planned to make my take off run a bit closer to the river, to avoid the center area of the bar, which had the consistency of talcum powder. Such a soft spot would be hard to see in any conditions, It was something to remember when looking over bush strips in the future. We did not need another problem with that soft center.

I cached all the shed antlers we'd picked up, along with the empty gas cans in a willow bush, planning to recover them at some later date.

Shadows were lengthening as we got ready. The engine started easily and I let it warm up for several minutes. When I went through the mag check at 1800 rpm, a little vibration was apparent, whereas normally there was none. I held the brakes and ran it up to 2200, still without too much shaking, so we back taxied to get all the usable length we could out of that twisted bar. When I turned, the tail wheel went into the water, maximizing the length of my runway. Next, I put the whip to it,—all twenty-seven hundred rpms.

The wind had picked up to about fifteen miles per hour coming right down the bar, which aided our take off and we were airborne in about eight or ten seconds. I leveled out, banked left and backed off the power to 2100 rpm at which setting the vibrations seemed least, and headed straight for Kotzebue.

We arrived just after dark, for which I was thankful, not wanting to advertise that I'd made such a stupid mistake. As soon as the Cub was secured in it's tie downs I took off the spinner, propeller and cowling and put them in my work shop. It was so good to be home with the airplane.

First thing the next morning, Nelson Walker was banging on our front door. When I opened it, he said "Ya wrecked yer airplane, didn't ya, Jake? I know how it is, didn't want anybody to know, did ya?"

I remarked that he really knew how to hurt a guy or something to that effect.

He said "I brought some bucking bars and a good ball peen hammer, so you can start pounding out the dents and get 'er smoothed out and painted up and be back in business."

I poured him a cup of coffee and thanked him profusely, as I had only a sand bag and a claw hammer for doing the sheet metal work.

He reminded me that I would have to replace the propeller and track it to be sure that the crankshaft hadn't been bent. I described how I had done that on the site and he said that technique would be good enough, but the prop was ruined and a new, full length propeller should be tracked anyway.

With a couple hours of pounding on the soft aluminum, followed by taping and spray painting, I had the cowling and a replacement prop back on the Cub that same evening. It seemed that the crank shaft was not bent so I flew it around the patch. The Cub performed beautifully—and with no vibration. Whew!

The Second Cub—Ground Loop In Galena

By 1976 I had sold the Cessna 180 and I was thinking I needed another plane to use on floats during the summer and skis during winter, so I could leave 21P on wheels the year around. Shellabarger told me that he would like to add a Cub on floats to his fleet.

So, on a trip to Portland, Oregon for my ten year dental school class reunion in April I happened to mention my plans to a friend who directed me to a place in Vancouver, Washington. There, in a warehouse was a brand new set of Edo 2000 floats with double water rudders, still in the crates. They would be ideal for a Super Cub. The owner was asking about half of the going rate for the floats, which was five thousand dollars, so I bought them on the spot and arranged for their shipment to Anchorage.

My return home to Kotzebue included an overnight in Anchorage which I spent with Jim and Joye Cann. Jim said that his old polar bear hunting partner had a Cub for sale. Jim also mentioned that a fellow (me) would have to keep an eye on any dealings with the owner of any used airplane. That Cub had been wrecked a few times but was a good airplane. It had double wing tanks in it, giving it about nine hours of flying time. I stayed an extra day to have a good look at it. It checked out, but needed an annual inspection. The price was ten thousand five hundred dollars—that same magic airplane price that I had paid for the Cessna and for my first Super

Cub. This Cub was N7156Z. I debated a few days, then called the owner and said I would take it, but only after it had an annual by a mechanic that was acceptable to both of us. Furthermore, I wanted to be present and assist in the annual inspection. The agreement was made and I was to go pick it up in about ten days.

When I returned to get the Cub, the annual had already been started, but was not yet been completed, so I participated in some of that work. One afternoon I got distracted by other business and was not present for some of the critical work and the final sign off. The brakes were inspected in my absence. And I did not give them a going over on my own. That was a foolish mistake on my part.

After holding for two days waiting for weather to improve enough for the VFR shot to Kotzebue, I loaded up early in the morning and struck off, headed through Rainy Pass, then to McGrath with a stop in Galena for a short bladder break.

The trip was somewhat turbulent, but otherwise uneventful, until I got to Galena. The U.S. Air Force controlled the Galena airport in those days. The control tower boys were accustomed to dealing with fighter jets that landed and took off at very high speeds and were less influenced by ground winds than a light STOL aircraft would be, so they paid less attention to winds of 15 or 20 mph than we who fly slower, less powerful machinery have to do.

I was given clearance to land heading down river, but that had an eighteen mile per hour quartering tail wind from the left and the paved runway was soaked from heavy rain. Not realizing that the ski strip which was dirt and therefore more forgiving than wet pavement on big tires was available, I accepted the clearance and resolved to fly the Cub onto the runway with more speed than normal—as would be necessary with such a tail wind.

Those were two major mistakes on my part—accepting the tail wind and not asking about an alternate runway or a dirt road to land on.

I got the main wheels down firmly on the runway, but as I reduced power to let the tail wheel come down, I suddenly began to weather cock, or ground loop to the left. I applied hard braking on the right, but the brake went limp. I felt nothing on that brake pedal. The right brake was completely soft and I did an abrupt ground loop which ended with my right wing slamming hard onto the pavement.

"7156Z, are you all right?," called the tower. I said that I was okay, but I was thoroughly disgusted. I deplaned, straightened the Cub out, and taxied to the ramp.

When I got out of the Cub again, I looked closely at the right wing. It was noticeably bent up at the outboard end. A mechanic from a nearby hanger came over and said that "would take some fixin."

I was sure that I saw dollar signs ringing up in his eyes and said I'd take care of it at home. He said "it would be too bad if the wing fell off on the way home, eh?"

Well, either I fly it home or the other option would be to leave the plane in Galena, for how long, I could only guess. It would be left in the hands of strangers, and I would have a huge bill to pay, no doubt. It was an uncomfortable moment of decision for me.

I wasn't going to let myself be hoorawed by any avaricious bush mechanic, especially one who looked like he wasn't busy, as this one did. I had a cup of coffee and a snack as I mulled over my situation. Then I decided I'd better fire up and get out of there as I had a fair piece—approximately two and a half hours of flying, yet to travel.

I called the tower, was given clearance to depart in the opposite direction from which I had landed and I rolled down the runway, into the wind.

When I broke ground, the plane wanted to roll to the right. It took full left aileron to hold it straight and level. Even then it was flying with the right wing low. It was not pretty, completely safe, or comfortable, but I made it to Kotzebue.

The next morning I got hold of Gene Starkweather to look at it. He was a pretty savvy field fixer upper and told me that I had a broken wing spar. We went to the local lumber supplier and after rejecting dozens, we found a fir two by four stud with tight grain and no knots. We stuffed that piece of lumber in alongside the damaged spar, strapped and taped it in place and I flew it that way for more than three thousand hours without a problem. That repair held through my flipping the plane upside down in the river, collapsing a gear on a ski take off and general hard bush use. It cost about two hundred dollars for the material including Gene's fee for the work and signing the log book, rather than several thousand

Edo 2000 floats are not heavy.

Moment of truth, suspended without undercarriage.

for a total wing rebuild, as would have been the case if I'd had left it to be done in Galena. I realized that I had been blessed throughout this entire experience.

In June, I flew 56Z back to Anchorage and together with Voight Clum, assembled the Edo 2000 floats. Then we changed the Cub from wheels to floats, loaded the wheels and gear in the back and I flew the seaplane to Kotzebue.

Now I had both 21P and 56Z leased to Shellabarger and 56Z was the only Cub on floats available for charter in Kotzebue. I kept busy with flying it on charters and gained a lot of experience in a hurry.

At freeze up I would use the community tripod and switch that Cub from floats to wheels, and soon thereafter to skis. In springtime it was back to wheels, then as soon as the lakes broke up, it went back on floats.

An interesting postscript: I traded N7156Z in 1986 for some property in Wasilla, Alaska, as I then had three Super Cubs and needed only two. The fellow who got 56Z let it sit unattended at Polar Airways on Merrill Field for two or three months, then one day he climbed in and took off. He hadn't checked the fuel level in the tanks or the position of the four way fuel selector valve. In fact he hadn't familiarized himself with the plane at all. The outboard tanks had very little fuel in them and he was running on one of those, rather than one of the main, inboard tanks. That's always a no-no from the get-go. One should always take off on the inboard tank with the most fuel.

When the engine stuttered, he did not think to attempt to switch tanks, which would have saved him—and prevented the wreck. He put the Cub down in a park area, but it sustained heavy damage. Luckily he was not injured. That was the only time he ever flew it. My mechanic friend, Voight Clum bought the wreck and called to tell me that the piece of two by four lumber was still fixed to the broken spar and serving well, but he was going to rebuild the wing, anyway.

Collapsing A Gear On Skis

My next "crash" actually began about a year before it happened. In April, I'd located a large collection of Arctic Hares on the Goodhope River south of Kotzebue on Seward Peninsula, and I made several trips to get some of those good eating, fun hunting, huge bunnies. On one trip, the snow had blown off of the frozen river, leaving it too rough to land on. The nearby lakes were also blown free of snow cover, but were smoother than the river.

A ski plane has no brakes and ground control is accomplished solely by the rudder and, when necessary, using the prop to send a blast of air over the tail and rudder to turn it. Of course juicing the throttle accelerates the plane, as well. Stopping comes without mechanical assistance of any kind and can take a long distance, especially on glare ice. On ice skates, a person can stop abruptly, but abrupt stops in a ski plane on ice are purely accidental and usually detrimental to the machine.

Well, I decided to put down on a narrow lake fairly close to one large aggregation of hares. The wind was a little stiffer than I had figured and it was coming directly across the lake. With no brake to keep the plane from weather cocking and too short a lake to correct with a blast of the throttle, I chopped the throttle and as we slowed down, I was soon sliding crosswise on the glassy surface. Near the end of the lake were some muskrat push-ups—hard icy lumps of about twelve to fourteen inches in height—and my right ski began hitting them. This resulted in putting hard impacts and adverse, lateral stress on the right gear.

When I got stopped, after my dog and I got out, I carefully checked the gear fittings. Not seeing any obvious damage, we went hunting. When we returned with 13 of the big hares, which weigh up to 17 pounds each, I looked the gear over again. My second inspection was more thorough than the first, but I detected nothing abnormal.

Taking off on glare ice is less hazardous than landing as the prop wash over the rudder provides good directional control which increases as the speed comes up. We lifted off easily without hitting any of the icy push-ups.

In late June, I switched the Cub from skis to floats and used it as a seaplane until early October, when it went back onto land gear. On all such gear changes, I carefully checked over the fittings, bolts, tubing, welds in the gear clusters, etc.

Then, the following February on a cold morning with the outside air temperature at about minus twenty degrees Fahrenheit, and once again on skis, I had loaded the Cub with dental gear for a trip to some villages and prepared to depart from the sea ice in front of my house. It was overcast with reduced visibility due to the leading edge of a storm system that was coming in from the north west. I wanted to get underway, bound for villages to the south, before the weather socked in and prevented my departure from Kotzebue. I figured the storm would last a few days during which time I could be settled into my field clinic in the first village and ready to move on to the next when the conditions improved.

The wind had picked up to about twenty-five miles per hour and it caused me to drift a little to the right of my intended run. The right ski impacted a small bump which is fairly common on skis, but it was enough to collapse the gear! The prop, turning at a full 2700 rpm struck the ice and the plane slewed to the right before the left gear let go. The engine quit after a couple of revolutions, but that was enough to twist the long Bohrer propeller beyond a repairable state. RATS!

No one saw the crash, except for me, of course. I got out, grabbed my most critical personal bag, which held my pistol. I took my rifle as well, and walked back to the house. I started the snow machine, unloaded the dental gear, survival gear and everything else into the sled and got all that stuff into the house. I called Leon Shellabarger and he said I'd better get the Cub into his hanger for whatever repairs were necessary.

The wind was increasing and carried snow with it. I unhitched the hardwood basket sled and hooked the snow machine up to my heavy freight sled, upon which I loaded an old mattress, some ropes, and my fuel pump, an empty fifty-five gallon barrel and several five gallon containers, then I called a couple of unemployed friends, asking them to come give me a hand getting the plane loaded onto the sled and into the hanger. While I waited for them to arrive, I set about pumping all the fuel that I could out of the four wing tanks into a barrel for later use in the trucks or snow machines. I wanted the aircraft to be as light as possible before lifting it from the ice. The tanks were topped off for the long trip and all together carried seventy-two gallons of eighty octane fuel which weighed four hundred and thirty-two pounds.

When my buddies arrived, I let them continue with transferring fuel from the four wing tanks into the barrel and five gallon containers, while I went out to the south runway to get the big pipe tripod. It took about an hour to locate the heavy tripod which had been completely covered by snow drifts, but I dug it out and loaded onto the freight sled to take to my

Collapsed gear—note the bent propeller!

wreck site.

My wife, Mae, closed up the store and came to help with removing the badly bent propeller and keeping parts and tools organized. In one photo she keeps hold of the left wing to make sure it doesn't hit the ice.

The freight sled sat low to the ice and getting the crippled plane on it was not too difficult, once I'd removed the gear and fuel. Using the tripod prevented more damage to the plane. Other than both gears and the propeller, there was no visible damage to the Cub. As we pulled the sled to the hanger, one man walked by each wing to stabilize the load.

Once we had the tripod and sleds at the site, things went pretty quickly. We had the Cub in the hanger before dark.

It's great to have friends like Leon and the others. Leon had experienced lots of wrecks of different types in a wide variety of circumstances. He surmised that so long as my crankshaft wasn't bent, my plane would be back in the air before the storm passed. However, as my prop struck the ice at full power, the possibility of a bent crankshaft was high.

We had to get the plane back on it's gear before we could track the prop so I was tense, wondering if the engine would have to be torn down and

The community tripod in use.

Getting the Cub ready to load on the sled.

Loaded onto the freight sled.

completely overhauled.

The forward right gear cluster was cracked and after I cut away the fabric I could see an old crack that had been there long enough to accumulate some rust. That likely took place when I slid sideways, hitting muskrat push-ups on the lake during the hare hunt ten months earlier.

The lesson from this wreck is: if one suspects damage to the gear fittings, always cut away the fabric and inspect it carefully with a magnifying glass. Fabric is inexpensive and easy to replace. Wrecks are never inexpensive or convenient.

I always kept at least one spare propeller in my warehouse The welding on the frame and gear cluster was done the first evening, allowing us to put the gear and skis back on. Tracking the prop had to wait until the next day. I slept uneasily.

First thing the next morning, I taped a sharp lead pencil to each blade of the prop and set a white piece of paper on a box beneath the prop such that the pencil would trace a line on it as each blade passed by. After both blades had rotated through, there was only one line marked. Great news! We did it again with the same result. This indicated there was no detectable damage to the crankshaft. Hallelujah!

The storm lasted four days, during which time I pecked around with little "tweaking projects" on 56Z. On the first good day, I pushed the Cub out of the hanger, test flew it, topped the fuel tanks off, loaded the dental gear and was on my way south.

September 10, 1983

That date is a tough one for me to write or think about, even after more than thirty years have passed since that fateful day. At first time seemed to drag on listlessly, but suddenly, before I noticed, time seemed to be rushing past faster than ever before.

I'll try to describe the unexpected chain of events that came our way.

When we returned to Kotzebue from our trip to Rhodesia—Zimbabwe in 1982, my wife, Mae, told everyone that she'd never had a better time than she had on that trip to the Dark Continent. We had shared many great times over our years together, some of which could be called adventurous, but this trip was tops.

In April of 1983, Mae began suffering from periodic bouts with blurred vision and severe headaches. After several episodes, and visits to the Public Health Service hospital in Kotzebue, without the doctors finding a cause, I sent her to Anchorage to see a private physician. No reason for her symptoms was discovered there either.

She got a new pair of eyeglasses which seemed to help.

We passed the summer doing our usual things with her running the store, and me doing dentistry, guiding and flying charters, along with our personal fishing, exercising the dogs and enjoying life. Things seemed warm, relaxed, and wonderful.

My Dad came up from Arizona in August to visit and help at the lodge, as he had done the two previous years. It was a wonderful privilege for us to be able to spend those special times together.

Peter Johnstone from Rhodesia—Zimbabwe was to have come in late August for his exchange hunt with us, but due to political problems at home, he had to cancel at the last minute. I had booked no other guests for that period. I was planning to do my best to show him as good a time as he had shown Mae and me the previous year, without the interruptions or distractions other guests would inevitably cause. So, with no opportunity to fill our prime vacancy with other hunting guests, my Dad, Mae and I, along with our labrador, Max, were the only ones at the lodge during what normally is the most beautiful and productive hunting time of the year.

Evenings we did some work on the lodge, building new bunk beds in the downstairs guest rooms, painting interior trim and other little home improvement projects.

On the afternoon of September 9 we spotted one caribou bull in a band of several dozen that had a great set of antlers, with exceptionally long back points that were well over eighteen inches in length—they were the longest that I had ever seen. Mae wanted to shoot it, but no opportunity could be found, as the animal remained in the middle of the herd, offering no clear shot. The band of caribou disappeared down the valley.

September 10, 1983

It's rare to ever see the same caribou two days in a row and by morning the valley was devoid of animals, except for a few gray jays and robins. After lunch Mae suggested that we should go looking for that outstanding bull, so we took the dog and got into the Cub. I doubted that we would actually find that same unforgettable animal, but we had the time and a beautiful day, so we went.

It was legal to take caribou the same day airborne in Alaska at that time.

About 20 minutes later, we found that unique bull in open tundra, feeding just off of the Kugururoruk River about eighteen miles downstream from the lodge. I landed on a short, curved bar and as we started after the bull, Mae told me that her headache had come back, but she wanted to get that animal. She had no trouble keeping up and soon she was offered a shot, and she put the bull on the ground. She mentioned again that she didn't feel great, so I hurried with butchering the caribou. We got back to the airplane and I loaded the meat and Max, tied the antlers on the right wing struts and then I noticed Mae sitting on a rock by the water's edge with her hands on the sides of her head.

Mae shot the big bull.

When I asked if she was okay, she said the headache was really bad. I asked if she wanted me to take her to the hospital, rather than back to the lodge.

She said, "just take me home, Jake, back to Trail Creek."

Still, more than thirty years later, I have a very painful time forcing myself to think of these events.

The wind was coming from the left quarter as I began the roll out from the gravel bar. When I came to the end of the strip, I pulled down full flaps and the Cub was airborne. I was holding left aileron into the wind and ready to slowly bleed off the flaps when the right rudder went limp to my feel and the Cub went into a slip toward the cut bank across the river. We were suddenly loosing altitude in the cross controlled situation. Apparently Mae had suffered a seizure and her right foot thrust forward, jamming the rudder pedal. I yelled "get off the rudder" and thought I could bring the nose up enough to get the plane over the top of the bank and into the waist high willows.

But we impacted just below the crest of the bank and I was thrown forward into the windshield. I woke up some time later suspended in my shoulder harness outside the right side of the windshield, with large snow flakes hitting my face. I could hear Max whining. My shoulder harness kept me from being completely ejected from the cabin. The right wing had struck the bank hard, driving the base of the wing into the cabin. Mae had been thrust forward as the wing root struck her head which drove her into the back of the pilot seat.

Just a few feet more would have put us into the willows.

I was aware of pain in my lower back, but I was focused on attending to Mae. When I got out, I helped Max get free, then was horrified at the sight of my wife. Her head and face were bloody. She was moaning as I struggled to unhook her seat belt and lift her free of the wreckage. I got her out of the aircraft and laid her on the ground. Then I carried her up the bank to a spot beneath some small cottonwood trees. I went back to the Cub for the tent and tarp, and turned my radio on. The radio lights indicated it was functional. I switched on the rotating red beacon and it worked, too, so I left it on, hoping for someone to see us.

By then large snow flakes were falling with more intensity.

After quickly erecting the tent I placed Mae inside with a sleeping bag around her. She was breathing, but did not respond to my pleading questions.

I placed a bottle of fresh water to her lips, but she took none. I pressed my check to hers and told her that I loved her.

She murmured "I love you."

After some time, I heard some deep gurgling sounds, then she stopped breathing. I tried giving her mouth to mouth resuscitation, but she did not respond and I could not detect her heart beat.

Words are insufficient to describe what I felt. I was stunned—devastated.

Some time after that, just before dark, I could hear an aircraft coming toward us, so I went to my aircraft radio. As another Cub flew by I called on the VHF guard frequency, 121.5. The Cub banked sharply and came by as the pilot asked "Jacob, is that you?"

"It's me. My wife is dead. I am okay, but I will need help," I responded.

I never did find out who that pilot was.

After a few hours (at the time, in my shocked state, it seemed like only minutes later) a helicopter arrived and took us to Kotzebue.

Our son and daughter, Martin and Sandy, met the chopper and both hugged me. I have never felt so low. I had lost my wife, as wonderful a mate

The Cub impacted the cut bank.

and companion as any man could ever have. I felt numb, empty, and worthless. Words are inadequate to describe my state.

Several friends were at our house when we arrived and two women friends spent the night there with me. A friend flew up to Trail Creek to give the awful news to my Dad, who said he would stay at the lodge until he heard from me. I did not sleep until some time the next day, and I did not sleep well for months afterward.

How could anyone's life be so horribly and abruptly changed?

Soon, I was tormented by an agonizing realization. Timing is so important. Anyone who drives a vehicle or flies an airplane has had near misses that, had they occurred a few seconds earlier or later, might have been disastrous. Conversely, in this case, Mae's seizure happened at precisely the worst possible moment. Seconds before, while still on the gravel bar or seconds later, with more altitude, there probably would not have been a crash. And she might have survived.

After a few days, I realized that my back pain was getting worse. I borrowed a steel corset brace and wore it during the day which helped, but I needed a constant flow of aspirin/codeine, which I sometimes augmented with whiskey, to keep me functional. An x-ray revealed that I had a double compression fracture of two adjacent lumbar vertebrae. I used that corset for about 6 months.

A couple of months after the disastrous accident I visited an acupuncturist, whose treatments gave me immediate, though temporary relief.

As soon as I could tolerate the motion, I began to exercise daily, and I have been able to get by very well, to this date, some thirty-plus years later.

Mae's autopsy showed that she had suffered a cerebral aneurysm, followed by severe trauma from the wreck.

We decided to scatter her ashes at Trail creek.

I needed to take the other Super Cub, N7156Z, off floats, but no one would tell me where the community tripod was located. It seemed no one wanted me to fly. Finally I located the tripod and made the gear change from floats to wheels without help from anyone. I chartered a Cessna to take Martin and Sandy to the lodge and we solemnly and tearfully scattered Mae's ashes on a nearby hill near a spot where we had done the same for several other people, most of whom had been our hunting guests.

I sent the chartered plane back to Kotzebue and remained for a while with our Labrador, Max, attempting to communicate with God. I pleaded with Him to give me a sign in a form that one so insignificant and unintelligent as I, could easily recognize. But I saw no such sign.

Max and I loaded up and started the flight back toward Kotzebue. At the mouth of Trail Creek, where it empties into the Kuguroruk River, permafrost on a large bluff was melting out. This is the kind of place where Mae and I had often found remains of wooly mammoths. She told me many times that we needed to keep an eye on that spot for a tusk. I teased her by saying that it was too far upriver and we'd never found any ivory there.

As Max and I flew by, I saw it! A white tusk had washed up on the bar downstream from the thawed area! The bar was a little rough and short, but I was determined to land.

When the tail wheel touched the gravel, the single bolt holding the tail spring in place broke and the rudder was in the gravel as we came to a stop. I retrieved the tusk and used it to hold the tail up as I considered how to fix it. The curved tusk was exactly perfect for its use as a stand for the tail of the Cub. I had no spare bolt, but I did have a large punch and some safety wire and tape which I used to hold the spring and tail wheel in place, at least temporarily. Using a modified soft field take off and landing technique, keeping the tail in the air as much as possible, my field repair was sufficient and no more damage was done. Ever since that day I have carried a spare bolt and nut in the Cub ... always.

A frost bank melting out.

A Sign

I believe that God had provided me with a sign I could recognize in form of the tusk. I related this series of events to my Dad and many others. Most of all, I thanked God! However the immediate relief that experience provided to my emotional condition was soon replaced by a serious and prolonged depression.

Most people treated me with great care and empathy. My freezer was over stocked with prepared meals. A flow of visitors from Fairbanks, Anchorage, Kotzebue, and surrounding villages kept me in nearly constant company, but I was severely lonesome and consumed with feelings of worthlessness, guilt, and despair. Sometimes grief overcame me and I burst into tears without apparent cause. I felt no shame at my bouts of crying.

Helpless as I felt, I laid awake thinking of what I could do to ease the misery that visited all of us, our family and friends, upon the loss of my wife. I began to cut an aluminum plaque, using my dental drill. I inscribed:

My Beloved Wife, Mae Jacobson, departed this world in this grove of poplars at 3:30pm on September 10,1983. No man ever had a better wife, partner and friend. Mae died at the end of a caribou hunt. She so loved this country, the animal life, hunting and fishing. Our separation, so painful now, is temporary. I love you, Mae.

— Jake

The wreck had occurred on National Park Service land and I was obliged to remove it as soon as possible. After scattering Mae's ashes, I went back to the wreck site to survey the situation. At that time I nailed the aluminum plaque on a cottonwood tree near the spot I had put up the tent and laid Mae. Then I began dismantling the wreck.

Our dog, Max, was a huge comfort to me. I spent most of my time at home, smoking cigars, drinking whiskey and stroking Max. My weight dropped from 175 pounds to 147 in four months. I never was much of a cook, but I'd always had a healthy appetite, until then.

My personal grooming, though never fastidious, had taken a nose dive. One evening in late November a female family friend came over and said that she was planning a party and I had to come. I told her that I just didn't feel like being around people. She said that I was, for sure, going to attend her party and if I didn't shave and clean up, she would bring a troop of women over to stick me in the bathtub, cut my hair and scrub me up. She ended by telling me that was not a threat, it was a promise. And she said, "By the way, your house stinks!" Stale cigar smoke permeated everything.

Others, including my very good friend, the local Jesuit Priest, cajoled me to get out and around people. With great reluctance, I allowed myself to be escorted to the party.

I felt weird and out of place. I had a hard time with even casual conversation with anyone. Many of the women asked me to dance. It seemed like everyone was handing me a drink and telling me a story. I was slowly

The cabin area of the Super Cub was badly smashed.

eased out of my extreme discomfort and actually found myself laughing, for the first time in months. The next morning, my feelings of guilt and emptiness returned, and they were intensified.

Being non gregarious by nature I was not a member of any clubs, but, similar to that first party invitation, I was almost forced by friends to attend a Lions Club meeting and I decided to join the organization. That same night I was asked to be Santa Clause for the community. With my long beard, it seemed a natural fit. I accepted the assignment, and found a Santa suit.

Listening to children's Christmas hopes and wishes was therapeutic for me. I would ask each kid if they were studying hard in school, if they brushed their teeth, if they minded their parents, etc. Of course, all professed to doing those things, all the time. I think every kid says, and believes he or she is a good kid when sitting on Santa's lap.

My good friend Hank Schimschat came by one Friday evening in December, trying to get me to accompany him to the bar, but I did not feel like doing that. So, he suggested that we take our snow machines and sleds the next day to hunt caribou on the Noatak River. I'd put up no meat for the winter, so I agreed to the trip.

Hunter Gone Berserk, or Poaching Hurts Us All.

We shot 3 caribou each before the few hours of daylight had vanished, and got them back to town well after dark. Remembering my Santa suit, I told Hank that we had an opportunity for a great photo. Next day, with my daughter, Sandy in the Santa suit, we three took a sled and some of the caribou to a suitable spot down the beach and I took several pictures, like the one above.

I was three months into what would be the loneliest, most empty time of my life, but I was slowly beginning to see that life could be worth living, again.

Upside Down In The Kuguroruk River

In September, 1983, in the process of recovering my wrecked Cub, N3421P, I dumped my second Super Cub, N7156Z, into the river. It flipped upside down as soon as the main wheels hit the water during my attempted take-off, and had floated down the ice choked stream until it hung up on a large rock. Simultaneously with grounding on the rock, a large piece of heavy floating ice smashed the clamshell window on the right side of the cockpit, allowing water and ice to quickly begin to fill up the interior, as I, hanging upside down in the seat harness in my heavy and now thoroughly soaked goose down parka, worked to release the harness buckle, to allow my escape. I got out, soaked, cold, and angry. I swam across one deep hole, but mostly waded back to the gravel bar from which I'd attempted the takeoff. In the main channel the river was waste deep, running with ice and a stiff current

This wreck was entirely due to pilot error—my own. And in part it was due to accepting the go ahead signaled by another fellow, also a pilot, who had accompanied me to the remote site to help in the recovery of my first wreck, N3421P. This was clearly an accident, not an incident.

It was a Friday and the fellow who flew his plane up with me to help strip usable items from the 21P wreck was a follower of the Seventh Day Adventist faith. He was strictly devout and observed the ethic of not working from sundown Friday until sundown Saturday. Weather had delayed our arrival at the wreck and by the time we were ready to return to Kotzebue, it was just about an hour before sunset. We had approximately an hour of flying between us and town. Barring unforeseen events, we might make it back to town by sunset, if we avoided delays. I was perhaps more concerned with not delaying my able helper past sundown, than he was.

Not what I had intended.

It looked really bad.

Snow began to fall and the flakes were large and sticky. After brushing snow from the top of the fuselage, the horizontal stabilizers and the elevators, I used a rope to clear snow from the wings and told my helper to look closely at the wings when I was ready to take off. If more snow was sticking to the top of the wings, I would need to clean them again. We might have to delay taking off until the conditions improved. We might have to spend the night, if necessary.

Relying on anyone else to inspect my wings was not good thinking on my part. I should have climbed out and looked them over myself. It mattered little to me if we needed to spend the night in the tent I always carried, but I wanted to accommodate my companion ... and I trusted him and his judgement regarding the presence of sticky snow on the wings, or lack thereof.

The usable part of the gravel bar was a bit rough and pretty short—maybe 400-450 feet in length. The wind was light, but I was not loaded heavy. I did the short taxi to the end of the "strip," held the left brake as I turned the plane into the wind, and made the question gesture to him. He gave me the 'both thumbs' up sign to go ahead. After the fact, I'm not sure he could clearly see the top and back of my wings.

I locked the brakes, applied throttle to near full and let go of the brakes. With the rocks and the uneven surface, acceleration was not the best, but it seemed adequate. At the end of the bar I pulled full flaps and was airborne, but the plane immediately began to settle, loosing what little altitude it had very rapidly. I had never experienced this situation before. I kept the nose low, but was headed for the middle of the river and soon was in it. Just before the wheels contacted the water I pushed forward a little on the stick, hoping to put the big main tires onto the surface at a low angle and remain airborne long enough to gain some speed, or at least reach the gravel bar across the river. but it did not help.

Instead of running across the surface of the river, when my tires contacted the water, the plane immediately nosed up and flipped over.

It happened so fast, but seemed to be taking place in slow motion as I lived through it. Each millisecond of the developing disaster seemed frozen in a muted, digitalized sequence to which I was merely a witness.

Enough snow must have stuck to the top surface of the wings to destroy lift and bring me down.

I was upside down, floating down the river amidst the broken ice pans until the plane struck a rock, skewed a bit and hung up on a mid stream gravel bar. About that time a large pan of ice broke the clamshell door window and water began to fill the cabin.

Once I was out of the plane, my reaction was pure anger. I was angry at myself for not checking the wings again—for leaving that critical determination to someone else. I normally never left important decisions that would affect me to anyone else to make.

The other fellow had some long ropes which we tied together with mine and I went back into the river, crossing to the opposite side to attach one end to the tail spring of the Cub. I was so concerned about loosing the second plane, I really didn't feel the cold from the icy water, though I was soaked and my hip boots were full. I tied the other end of the rope to a cottonwood tree and squeezed some of the water out of my parka. The snow had stopped falling.

Then after thoroughly roping the snow off his wings, we both got into his plane and he flew us back to Kotzebue.

Darn! Timing is everything they say. Had I gone before the brief, sticky snowfall or just a half hour or so later, when the snow had stopped, I would have had no problem. Had I checked the wings myself, I likely would not have wrecked the plane.

In Kotzebue the next day we loaded a replacement propeller, twenty gallons of gas, seven quarts of oil, a half dozen large spray bottles of WD40 and other recovery supplies, and went back to the now double wreck site in his plane. The river had gone down significantly overnight. We used my three-eights inch rope come-a-long, attached the rope to the tail spring and brought my Cub up and over to a three point posture in the water, then I pushed and pulled the aircraft while the other fellow winched it ashore. Wearing a borrowed pair of chest waders, I did not get very wet during my work in the river this time.

Once the plane was out of the river, we removed the spark plugs, turned the prop through several cycles by hand and were amazed and relieved to find that no water had gotten into any of the four cylinders. I sprayed the inside of the cylinders and the rest of the engine liberally with WD-40. We carefully sprayed the plugs with WD40, then cleaned and dried them and

The next day, bringing N7156Z upright with a come-along.

Ready to push and winch the Super Cub
ashore.

screwed them back in place.

With the replacement propeller installed we taped a pencil to each tip and turned it through so the pencil would mark a piece of cardboard. Both tips traced the same, so it appeared the crank shaft was not damaged or bent.

We drained the fuel and hopefully all the water from the four wing tanks and placed ten gallons of new gasoline in each inboard tank, then carefully checked for water. The quick drain showed no water, so we were ready to try to start the engine. The temperature was plus twenty-six degrees.

Three shots from the primer and the engine coughed and sputtered. After a few minutes contemplation and some discussion, three more shots from the primer and it fired up and ran smoothly! What a blessed relief that was.

Amazingly enough, the damage to the light plane was minimal. No control surfaces were damaged, but as the plane had been totally submerged, I paid special attention to all control surface hinges, spraying them liberally with WD40. The broken side window was replaced with cardboard for the trip to town, which made the hour long transit to town less drafty, but it was not absolutely necessary. Luckily the greenhouse roof and windshield were intact. After application of duct tape to several areas, it looked like my Cub was ready to fly.

It was now about an hour after the initial engine start and no water was showing in the sump. The second start was immediate and smooth, so I warmed it up for another five minutes until the cylinder head and the oil temperatures were well above one hundred degrees. I took every precaution I knew to insure that a repeat of the previous day's abysmal performance would not occur. I was resolved to make sure I got airborne and all the way home this time.

I taxied the Cub to the same spot of my disastrous take off of the previous day, locked the brakes, slowly pushed the throttle full forward and released the brakes. The Cub was as light as possible and it rolled out nicely this time. Coming to the end of the bar I had a fleeting bit of apprehension, but when I popped full flaps, my machine leapt into the air. This time it felt solid and did not settle. And I thanked God!

The return trip to Kotzebue was uneventful, as was the landing.

I taxied the plane up to my good friend Leon Shellabarger's heated hanger, pushed it inside, and let it sit for two days, on his recommendation, to let it "pee all the water out." I drained all four fuel tanks—saving that gas for use in the pickups or snow machine after filtering. I thoroughly flushed the aircraft fuel cells and lines several times, then I topped the tanks off with filtered aviation fuel.

All things considered, this time, I was very, very lucky. I knew I had been flying in the palm of God's hand.

Water Skiing

My old friend Art Fields took me back to the wreck site to remove the engine and other salvageable parts from 3421P. We wrapped the engine in a canvass secured by ropes and stashed other parts in the brush. The wings, rudder, horizontal stabilizers and elevators were carefully removed and stowed in the willows nearby, to be picked up as soon as possible and taken to town.

We loaded the radios and instruments in the back of Art's Cub, and we were ready to depart after about four hours of work.

The little portion of that gravel bar suitable for landing was rough, short and curved, but I'd been on it several times without mishap and Art was a very experienced Cub jockey. It seemed to be a routine takeoff in the making. However, a breeze of about fifteen miles per hour was directly across the strip. At the water's edge, Art popped the Cub off the ground with full flaps, but we began to settle back onto the river—it was a dreadful deja vu experience similar to the one I'd had with 56Z a few days before. I was braced and anticipating a watery flip over. Just before touching the water, with full throttle still engaged, Art pushed his stick forward driving the tires onto the water more forcefully than my attempt to do so, and we ran across the surface of the river with those big tundra tires throwing up rooster tails behind us. Art turned a bit to the left to extend his run on the river before gaining enough speed to depart the liquid surface. He let his wheels bounce two times on the bar across the river, then pulled back on the stick and we were once again flying. Our passage was wobbly and mushy, but we remained airborne.

Art turned back to look at me and said "Hey, Jacob, wanna go water skiing? Maybe we been missing some fun, huh?"

Flying A Twin Engine Super Cub

I got back to the crash site when weather improved a few days later with my son, Martin, who helped me load the engine of N3421P into the back seat of N7156Z and tie it down securely. Leaving Martin with the tent, food and a rifle, I took the engine back to Kotzebue.

So I got to fly a twin engine Super Cub for the first time. Believe me, they fly better with a single engine!

I unloaded the engine and other parts of 21P by myself and went back to get Martin. We stopped by the mouth of the Kuguroruk River and, in thirty minutes, caught a half dozen sea-run arctic char for home use.

Step by rigorous step, we were getting the two wrecks attended to as well as could be done.

The wings of 21P remained stowed in the willow brush at the crash site. I wanted to get them to town as soon as possible before some grizzly wandered by and decided to chew them to pieces. So at the first decent break in the weather I went back to the site with the friend in his Cessna 180 to load and secure the wings under the belly of his plane for transport to Kotzebue.

The carcass of 21P was to sit at the wreck site until March, 1984, when two of my friends -Hank Schimschat and Larry Lewis got to it with snow machines and equipment to remove the big tires and install skis which were put on backwards, as the easiest way to transport a Cub like that was by hauling it tail first behind a sled. They made the round trip in two days.

I had broken my left foot and ankle in early March and was wearing a cast at the time or I would have been along for the retrieval of the fuselage. They made a fine recovery for me, traveling down the Kuguroruk River to the Noatak and then on to Kotzebue—a distance of more than one hundred and sixty miles over ice and snow.

Back in town, when we did a careful inspection of the fuselage, it looked like I would be better off to just buy another one. The "N" number was about all that was worth saving from that part of my wreck.

Mayday

In the meantime I was scheduled to make a couple of dental field trips to some villages in the Norton Sound area which is part of the Bering Sea, lying to the east and a little bit south of Nome. When I penciled out the costs of chartering for the entire trip or flying by jet to Nome with hotel

Wings of 21P loaded under fuselage of the Cessna 180.

and taxi costs, then on mail planes to the villages, it appeared that costs of that form of transportation would consume all my expected profits, or maybe even more. I'd left 56Z on big tires that winter, as my zeal for outdoor activity was dampened by my general depressed state of spirit and the leg cast. Tires were best for village trips, as by that time most little communities were able to keep their runways clear with graders.

With skis, no brakes are used, but tires often require the use of brakes and I couldn't reach the left heel brake with the cast on my left ankle and foot, so I used my dental drill to split the fiberglas cast down each side and leave it off when flying. I could quickly use duct tape to put it back in place when I got out of the plane. I felt pain when applying the brake with no cast in place and this activity retarded the healing, but it allowed me to fly myself and gear for the winter dental trips.

I visited Elim first, then flew down to St. Michaels. The activity irritated my left ankle, but aspirin/codeine kept the pain tolerable. Immediately after landing I would take out a roll of duct tape, strip off my bunny boot and tape the fiberglas cast back on the left ankle. Over the cast I wore a caribou

The fuselage of N3421P was too hammered to repair.

skin sock that kept my foot warm until I could get inside a building.

It was a normally cold winter and the ocean was frozen of course, making a vast expanse of snow on thick sea ice, broken in places by pressure ridges. Most of the surface was too rough to land a plane on, but some larger pans were reasonably smooth and could accommodate a light aircraft landing on skis or even wheels if necessary. However in bright sunlight the smooth pans produced a glare which was hard on the eyes, even with sunglasses. The glare made detection of potentially dangerous cracks and ridges difficult.

It was about zero degrees Fahrenheit and blowing a pretty strong cross-wind when I departed St. Michaels, headed for Kotzebue. It was a darned good thing I had the cast off, as I had to use heavy left braking to hold the plane straight down the runway. Once airborne I reduced power and trimmed the plane for the best rate of climb at seventy-two miles per hour and was just off Egg Island at three thousand, two hundred feet and climbing when my engine suddenly quit.

Immediately my left hand went to the fuel selector valve. That Cub had four wing tanks and a four-way fuel selector valve. I had taken off and was running on the right inboard tank. Each inboard tank was more than half full. But I couldn't move the selector valve lever.

Apparently there was still some water somewhere inside the fuel system from its dunking in the Kuguroruk River more than seven months earlier, and that water had finally made its way to the selector valve and then frozen in that restricted part of the line. I had cabin heat on full and put both cabin heater hoses next to the valve before I called Nome on a MAYDAY, giving my position just southeast of Egg Island. I also told them that I thought I could land on wheels on a flat stretch of ice below me and was going to continue to circle within gliding distance of that flat pan. I added that soon I would be on the east side of Egg Island and unable to communicate with Nome radio.

In the meantime I kept trying to get the fuel selector valve to function. With the engine not running, the heat coming from the hoses was rapidly diminishing.

I said a quick prayer which ended with me telling God that, once again I realized that I was entirely in His hands.

On the lee side of Egg Island I found calmer air, assuring myself that the landing should not be too difficult.

I kept trying to move the fuel valve lever. Even through my gloves, I thought it began to feel warm. Then I felt the valve lever give a little and with another effort I was able to switch it to left main tank. The propeller was windmilling and within seconds the engine coughed and fired up. It stuttered a little, probably due to a some water in the carburetor, then it caught and ran smooth.

An aircraft engine had never sounded better to my ears!

I was below 600 feet when I got the engine restarted. I flew out from behind the Island and called Nome to advise them of my improved situation and that I was going to stay there, making slow climbing turns, until I got at least 3,500 feet, before heading directly to Unalakleet. I also told them to close my flight plan to Kotzebue as now I planned to spend the night in Unalakleet.

After landing at the village without a problem, I taxied over to the Ryan hanger and got out. I taped my cast back in place as I sat on the tire. Wilfred Ryan Sr. had heard my Mayday transmission and my follow-up call. He walked over and told me to put my plane in his hanger overnight which he kept at about 50 degrees to be sure there was no more water in the fuel system. Wilfred had to move one of his own airplanes out of the hanger to make space for mine inside. I gladly accepted his kind offer and called a school teacher friend named Jack Wilfong, with whom I spent the night.

I am certain that the water in the fuel line was left over from the dousing in the river back in the previous September. I had drained the lines, flushed them three times, and had flown the airplane on several trips since it had been submerged, but still, enough water was hiding somewhere to nearly cause me grief.

My prayers that night were primarily those of intense and humble gratitude.

Winning N8102Y

Throughout most of my life, I've been blessed with the comforting belief that I'm a lucky guy. More than that, I believe I have been blessed. So many times, had things happened mere seconds before or after they occurred, my situation would have been much worse, maybe even debilitating or fatal.

Clearly, I'd rather be lucky and blessed than smart, but being both would be my preference.

I had an instance of something far worse than bad on September 10, 1983 which I wrote about in another story. Timing clearly did not favor us that day.

The following spring I was in Anchorage doing a lot of things, including searching for a replacement fuselage for my wrecked Super Cub, N3421P. I stopped by Stoddards Aircraft Parts and asked my long time friend, Bill Robek if he knew if any fuselage in decent condition was available.

"Jake, I don't know of any, but here, buy a ticket and win the Super Cub parked across the street. Tickets are only twenty bucks and it's for a good cause—the Alaska Libertarian Party," Bill said as he shoved a book of raffle tickets across the counter to me.

Across the street sat a white Super Cub. It looked like a clean airplane, a dandy, really, but I wasn't feeling at all lucky.

I told Bill that it hadn't been a good day for me. I had been given a ten dollar ticket for an expired parking meter. I arrived at my rental car just as the meter maid began to fill out the citation. She acted like she couldn't hear me explaining that I had been held up due to another lady's panicky kid getting his shoe lace caught between a display cabinet base and the floor at Penny's department store. I helped get the young boy on his feet and had to use my pocket knife to cut the shoe lace, which was irretrievably jammed, so he could put his shoe back on and get on with life, which for the moment was to stop crying. Then he could continue shopping with his Mom. I told the meter gal that we could probably find the pair to verify my story just inside Penny's, but she just kept filling out the ticket, avoiding eye contact. When she handed it to me, she lifted her head and looked at me with an unemotional, corpse-like gaze. She never uttered a single word. A real nice gal she was. She might have been a zombie!

I felt like I was participating in a horror movie at midday.

From there, I had made a brief stop at the La Mex restaurant for a quick plate of enchiladas, telling the waitress that I was in a hurry. After being assured that the meal would be forthcoming in just a few minutes, it was handed to another guy, who unknowingly ate my lunch. I was rushed and so I had to do without lunch.

It clearly just wasn't my day.

But my friend Bill had thrust a stack of tickets in front of me and I noticed that the top one was numbered 3421 which was the number of my wrecked Super Cub! I told Bill that since that number was so familiar and significant to me, I would buy that one ticket. He said, they were twenty dollars each and six for a hundred bucks. I told him that was the only ticket I would need and he could just call me to let me know that I'd won the Cub after the drawing result was made known on the Fourth of July.

I filled out the ticket, put the stub in my wallet, and thought no more of the matter.

That same trip, I found another wrecked Super Cub up by Palmer, the wings of which were trashed, but the fuselage was practically untouched. I bought it and arranged to have it flown up to Kotzebue on a freighter.

N3421P was on her way to her restoration ... or perhaps, her resurrection.

The Fourth of July, 1984

On the evening of the third of July my labrador, Max, and I were home alone in Kotzebue when my good buddy, Hank Schimschat, called. He wanted to borrow some moose and caribou racks to use on a float he was building for the parade. I said he could come over and pick whatever he wanted. He was at my place minutes later. After we loaded the antlers on his truck, he insisted that I accompany him to the favorite local bar, the Ponderosa, for at least a couple of beers. I resisted, but Hankeroo is a persuasive guy, so I gave in and was soon sipping a cool beer when I noticed a very attractive young woman that seemed to be eyeballing me. Next thing I knew, she came over and told me it was lady's choice and asked if I would dance with her.

Well, dance we did, and we enjoyed a most interesting and memorable evening.

The Fourth of July is always a big event in Kotzebue and I attended the parade and partook of several delicacies offered by the local food vendors. It was windy and chilly that day when the lady I met the night before asked if I might have a fur hat she could borrow. Well I had one—a warm and appropriate piece of apparel for her to display in her capacity as judge of the beauty contest. She should make a good judge, as she, herself, was a beauty.

Dutifully, I went home to get the red fox hat for her to use. I noticed that my answering machine was blinking—indicating that it held a new message.

I hit the button and heard the announcement that I had won the Libertarian Party Super Cub. Wow! But reality trumped my elation as I convinced myself that my friend Bill Robek had probably made the call to hoorah me.

But I hit the button again and realized that it was not Robek's voice and the announcement gave my ticket number. Weak knees followed on the heels of a huge adrenaline rush. I began to believe that indeed, I had won that airplane. I listened to the recording a third time and wrote down the number to call for confirmation of the win. With trembling hands and limp fingers, I dialed the number.

The Cub was mine! I had actually won that Super Cub!

That, on top of the fascinating lady I met the night before was too much to believe. I sat down on the couch, with my labrador, Max in my lap and just stroked his head and stared at the ceiling. And I thanked God.

After an indeterminable period of time in my stunned ecstasy on the couch, I realized that I should return to the festivities with the fur hat, so I gave Max a short run outside to relieve himself, then I embraced my pooch in another big hug before I rushed back to the stunning selection of gorgeous Miss Kotzebue contestants. I would not have been a good judge that day, as due to my recent experiences, absolutely everything I saw looked perfectly beautiful to me.

I called my mechanic friend, Voigt Clum, in Anchorage, and asked that he take possession of the Cub, N8102Y, for me, move it to a tie-down at Polar Airways and give it an annual inspection before I went down to Anchorage to pick it up and fly it home to Kotzebue.

N8102Y was a clean airplane, having been kept up to date mechanically and paper-wise. It had been hangared in Montana, prior to being purchased and flown to Anchorage for the drawing. However, it had no landing or taxi lights, so I asked Voight to put both lights in the left wing as per the standard installation mode. The radios were not the best, but they seemed to check out, so I could deal with that situation by replacing them as opportunities and finances allowed.

In late July, I took my new lady friend to Anchorage to pick up the Cub. This lady, though born in Kotzebue, had been living a very urban lifestyle in the "South-48." She was enthusiastic about my "rough shirts and lifestyle," but had not experienced many of the things that she would soon have to endure, and try to learn to like, if she was to keep company with me.

We loaded the plane and struck off for Kotzebue one rainy morning. Weather looked grim in the more southerly routes, so I filed a flight plan that would take us up the Parks Highway, through Windy Pass, north to the Yukon River, then down stream to Galena, where I would top off the fuel tanks. This Cub had a factory installed eighteen gallon tank in each wing. From Galena I planned to fly directly on the Victor Airways, V498 route, taking us over the mountains, crossing the Gisasa and Kateel Rivers and into the Tagagawik and Buckland drainages. The last leg should keep us in the air for around two or two and a half hours.

But, the rain intensified and was accompanied by fog. On the north side of Windy Pass I set the ADF (automatic direction finder radio) for Galena. We followed the needle and found ourselves at Lake Minchumina. That ADF was definitely not reliable.

I turned north and immediately recognized the mighty, forever muddy, Yukon River when we reached it. Galena was right there waiting for us and my thirsty wing tanks were soon filled.

Forecasts were for marginal VFR conditions which is usually plenty good enough to fly safely, so we departed, bound for Kotzebue. When we reached the Koyukuk River, I decided to follow it upstream until I could find better conditions for a more direct shot through the Purcell Mountains and on toward home.

Weather didn't look great, but with four and a half hours of fuel now aboard, I decided, as soon as we saw a chance, to try to punch through to the head of the Selawik River and fly on to the west, and home.

The rain did not let up so we followed the meandering loops of the Koyukuk for nearly two hours in slow flight with flaps down due to the limited visibility which had deteriorated to one mile and less, in places. When we got to the north side of Roundabout Mountain, I decided we should land at Huslia and wait out the weather. Using the new plane with its standard fuel tanks, too much more looping around could run us dangerously low on gas. I'd already burned up more than a third of my fuel and still had ninety percent to the distance to travel, so I landed.

A great airplane for twenty dollars!

For years I had heard some horror stories about bad treatment of small planes and pilots that landed in Huslia, but landing there was our best option. I landed easily on the state maintained gravel field and immediately two men came to meet us. The older fellow began the conversation, asking my intentions. I told him that we would have to stay until the weather improved, but I had a tent and food. He suggested that we take advantage of the local village owned lodge, for which we could pay thirty-five dollars per day and use the food available on the shelves, paying for it on an honor basis. That sounded better than a tent in the stormy weather, especially considering I had a female companion. The old gentleman also told me that there were some real ornery young fellows in that village, so he suggested that I leave the door of the plane open to discourage any would-be break-ins, and take all our stuff with us to the lodge. He also told me that he would put the word out that we were friends of his and that being done, it was not likely that anyone would bother the airplane.

Of course I had my pistol, but I did not show it. That fine older gentleman brought a wheel barrow to help us get our load of stuff to the lodge and he stopped by to visit several times in the next three days as we waited out the storm. We enjoyed a nice evening meal at his home followed by cookies fresh out of the oven, made by his wife. After dinner we engaged in some card games.

After three days and nights of reading books and watching the weather, the nasty overcast relented, partial clearing came, and we flew on to Kotzebue in the new airplane.

It was normally only about two and a half hours from Huslia on to Kotzebue, but a direct shot was not possible, so when we landed in Kotzebue, I didn't have that much fuel to spare. Only about thirty minutes of flying time remained. But we got home with the airplane.

This plane too, was a very good performer, primarily due to the rigging, which a good Super Cub mechanic should be able to do well, but it seems few have the special talents of a first class rigger. Luckily, I knew such a fellow who helped me with that. Things to consider in rigging are that one gets the maximum cruise speed by having all control surfaces line up to minimize drag. Wing dihedral should be such that the wing tips point slightly higher than the roots. The opposite, anhedral, or drooping wings can improve the performance, but results in reduced cruise speeds. The stall should not be abrupt and vicious, putting the Cub into a spin upon reaching full stall. I checked these and other features and characteristics out carefully. The stall was gentle and, after a little tweaking—the other aspects were correct.

This Cub performed better than N7156Z, whose double wing tanks made it a bit "doggy." I needed extra fuel capacity for charter flights, so the next week, as I had done with 21P, I ordered a Cunningham thirty-two gallon belly tank for N8102Y. The belly tank actually made the Cub about two to three miles per hour faster on cruise and the extra range made its cost more than worthwhile.

I put my Edo 2000 floats on the new Cub and later sold N7156Z.

N8102Y served me well on wheels and floats until I swapped it for a boat, which I call *Lady Sasquatch*, and some money to boot in 1998. The wings and fuselage had required recovering during my ownership, but the 150hp Lycoming engine was unchanged and running fine when I traded it.

Winning that Super Cub came at a critical time for me and was one of the luckiest events in my life.

IPECAC and the Aircraft Mechanic

I n 1989 the mechanic I was using at the time told me that the wings of the Super Cub that I used on floats, N8102Y, needed to be recovered. That was the airplane I won in 1984 on a single twenty dollar raffle ticket. The fabric was the original cotton and had "ring wormed" pretty noticeably. This mechanic had been doing my annual and hundred hour inspections since we both worked for Leon Shellabarger in Kotzebue. I trusted him and agreed that the wings needed new skin.

His name was, curiously enough, Sharpe (or something similar), but other pilots called him Captain High Pitch, as his voice would go up a few octaves when he got excited, which was fairly frequent.

I flew both cubs—one at a time, of course—to his place outside Fairbanks in October to winterize them and tie them down in a hayfield near his shop. I had plenty of time before I needed to head down the road to Kodiak, so I suggested that we pull the wings off before I departed. For two men, removing the wings of a Super Cub is a simple job which can be done in two or three hours. But no, he said he wanted to keep on cutting his winter firewood. I insisted that we take the time to remove the wings and then store them in a protected place until he could start the fabric work. I had some float plane bookings scheduled for late June, 1990 that I didn't want to loose due to the Cub not being ready. He said "Trust me, Jake. It will be ready in early June."

Never trust someone who insists, or even suggests, that you trust them.

Right then, I should have taken the plane somewhere else, but I only raised my eyebrows and emphasized that I needed it in early June. He assured me, profusely, that the Cub would be ready.

"Trust me," he said again. Yeah, right. I was even more uneasy at his second suggestion to trust him.

So, in early June I arrived in Fairbanks and drove out to the hayfield to find my two airplanes tied to their stakes, just as I had left them the previous October. They had apparently been untouched since I had last seen them eight months before. Rats! The wings were still on N8102Y and they had not been recovered. I got hot!

When the mechanic came home I was sitting in my camper, parked in his yard.

I reminded him that I needed the wheel plane as soon as we could complete the annual inspection and the float plane soon thereafter. He again tried using that "trust me" bit. I was not calmed down at all, and I sure didn't trust him.

We got the annual done on the wheel plane, N3421P, in one day and I departed for Kotzebue, after Sharpe assured me that the wings and annual on the other Cub would be done by June 21. We'd already agreed on the price, so if he needed to hire more people to help work on it, that didn't matter to me. Sharpe was basically honest, but Shellabarger, too, often had to get after him to be punctual about getting airplane projects done on time. Leon would approach him in a threatening manner, with his hands ready to choke Sharpe and his face twisted into a maniacal grimace. Sharpe would take notice, his voice would go up a couple of octaves, and then he would get right to work.

For the next two weeks, each time I got back into Kotzebue from the lodge, I would call Sharpe for an update on the fabric work. Each time he said it was coming along fine and would be ready on time. But when I called on June 19, Sharpe said that he was running a little late, so he suggested that I come over to help. I let him know that I wasn't happy, but I would get a ticket on a commercial carrier and be there the next day. I emphasized that I needed, and intended, to fly that plane home as soon as possible.

I contacted the people who wanted me to do the float plane work and told them of my situation, adding that I was going to try to get it ready, but really could not guarantee it on time. I hated to do that. The job would bring in over $12,000 in revenue—far more than the cost of recovering the wings. I had no reasonable choice, but to inform them of the very real risk of delay. They did not confirm one way or the other if they would wait to hear from me on the availability of the plane. Their project also had a restricted time frame in which to be completed.

It was Friday noon, when I arrived at Sharpe's place. The right wing was completed, but the left side was just stripped and primed, with the fabric yet to be put on. Man, was I angry! He suggested that I could help best by sanding and painting the wing struts. I said, "Sure, where are they?" But, Sharpe couldn't find them!

After looking all around the shop, I went back to the hayfield, which was being mowed that afternoon. Sure enough, all four struts were lying in the uncut hay, about to be cut up and included in the cow feed. If I had arrived fifteen minutes later, they probably would have been diced up by the mowing machine, run over by the tractor, and ruined. That would have been another several hundred dollars expense, plus the time delay in getting replacement struts shipped to Fairbanks. I was mad enough to jam them all up Sharpe's backside. I told him that, and that he would not be going to work at his regular job until my Cub was reassembled, the annual inspection was completed, and the Cub was ready to fly. He seemed to sense my displeasure and immediately agreed (in high pitch) to my terms. He nodded his head in a rapid cadence.

That evening I called the project people to try to delay the float plane trips by three days or more, but they had already found another pilot and plane available during their time window who was willing to do the job. There went a large part of my annual income, right into thin air!

With Sharpe being even more disorganized than usual, I had to make several trips to town for parts, etc. I told him that if I caught him out of the shop or off his property, I would hang him on the spot. I remembered to mimic Shellabarger's choke grip, for Sharpe to see. I think he believed me.

It was warm and dry—perfect conditions for doing fabric and dope work—so the job should have and could have progressed rapidly.

Well, we both worked fast and effectively, the fabric was put in place, stitched, and painted, but by Sunday night, the plane was not yet ready. I reminded him that he wasn't going to his regular work until my job was completed. He silently nodded his head, but I suspected he was thinking otherwise.

That night I moved my camper to a little copse of spruce and birch trees on a one lane dirt road near the back entrance to Sharpe's place to intercept him if he tried to sneak away to his day job in the morning.

Moving to the highway to take off.

Early the next morning I was up sipping my coffee when along came Sharpe in his truck. He came around a brushy corner and was shocked to see me standing there, blocking his exit.

Knots had fascinated me long before I got into Boy Scouts and I had made up a hangman's noose. I got hold of Sharpe as he sat in his truck with the window down and had the noose around his neck before he could react. He started screeching as I opened the door and pulled him out of the seat, telling him that someone was going to find his limp, maggot infested body, rotting and twisting in the breeze.

He said "Jake, wait! I've got Ipecac!"

I said, "So what? What's the Ipecac for?"

He told me that he was going to drink some before he got to work and then throw up, so he could come home sick, with the boss's blessing.

My reply was to heck with that, just call in from here and don't waste time.

He argued that his financial security depended on that job. I countered that whether he had any sort of future or not was directly linked to getting my job done, too.

But, I relented, promising him that if he wasn't back before noon, I would hunt him down and hang him right on the spot, where ever I found him. Any telephone pole in Fairbanks would do just fine.

N8102Y on floats in Fairbanks.

He mentioned that he didn't know how much Ipecac to take, so I told him to drink half the bottle. He gagged it down.

Then I let him go, albeit with strong misgivings and censurable language.

I stayed busy with little projects that could have gone undone, until he drove up about noon. He did not look well. I asked him what had happened.

He said he didn't feel too good as he had thrown up two times on the road to Fairbanks. Fearing his gut was empty, he ate a McDonald's Big Breakfast before going to work. Choking back another heave, he walked into the boss's office, threw up on the desk and was sent home to recover.

My response was that he better recover fast and well enough to get my project done.

I've always been unsympathetic to what I perceive to be self induced problems.

I poured ten gallons of car gas into the left wing tank and ran the engine up on the ground. It seemed to be running fine. I liked the look of the fresh brown paint on the wings.

That evening we had the plane together and towed it from his place to the highway. This necessitated cutting some trees and brush on both sides of the dirt road from his place to the main thoroughfare. I wanted him in the back seat for the test flight—in case anything went wrong, but he had to block traffic, so I flew it alone. A bus full of tourists seemed entertained by this little scenario of life in bush Alaska, I saw many hands waving as I flew by a few feet over their heads.

I put the Cub through all the turns, slips, and stalls. It performed in fine shape, so I landed on the freshly cut hayfield and figured I'd head over to Kotzebue the next morning. Once there I could switch from wheels to floats.

I'd long since firmly resolved to find a different mechanic for the next year's annual inspections.

There was enough fuel in the left tank (the belly and right tank were bone dry) to get to Fairbanks International Airport where I topped off both wing tanks as well as the belly tank with its thirty-two gallon capacity and checked to be sure the hand pump was transferring belly fuel into the left main fuel cell. The old hand operated wobble pump, which had originally been in a World War II bomber, was functioning well.

As always, I began the trip on the left main tank. Then after six minutes I switched to the right main. In less than one minute after switching tanks, and bound for Kotzebue, the engine quit. I switched back to the left main and the windmilling engine fired right up, running smoothly. Lucky for me, that hand wobble pump transferred fuel from the belly tank into the left main and it continued to work just as it should. I got as high as cloud cover allowed—to about 8,500 feet—picked up a little tailwind and made it to Kotzebue with the belly tank empty and a little fuel to spare in the left main. The right main tank was full and still not flowing into the carburetor.

I spent the next day pulling the right main tank out of the wing after draining it of its nearly full eighteen gallons of gas. Once I had the tank out I found the remains of a rodent or bird nest clogging the drain hole. I cleaned the tank up thoroughly, flushed it several times, then flushed and checked its lines and filters all the way to the carburetor for sediments. That tank and the airplane performed fine from then until I traded the plane for a boat in 1998.

What a fiasco, but it could have ended in a real disaster from several aspects. I found a new mechanic to do my annuals the following season.

How I do love those supplemental belly tanks.

Second Engine Failure

Friendships Outlast Engines

Flying over water or terrane far from a safe landing strip, especially in adverse weather, sometimes causes strange sensations in the mind ... and sometimes ears, of pilots and passengers.

Small single engine airplanes are by far the most common aircraft in use throughout the world. The small twins usually don't have enough power with either engine to sustain more than an extended glide to the surface if one power plant fails, thereby dou-bling the chances of an engine failure, or so it seems to me. All but thirteen hours of my more than ten thousand hours as pilot in command on bush flights in Alaska have been in single engine aircraft.

N3421P after a paint "rejuvenation" in 2001.

After my first engine failure on Alaska's North Slope in June, 1976, I flew another seven thousand hours or so without any serious mechanical problems. I never worried much about it. Then, in 1999, it happened again, but that time I had been forewarned.

As had been my practice since selling my home in Kotzebue in 1986, I flew my aircraft to Fairbanks to tie down and store for the winter, then I did the annual inspection the following July or August and flew them back the four hundred and forty GPS miles to Kotzebue for use in the guiding operation. When guiding season was done, I flew the planes back to Fairbanks. In 1999 I followed that same routine.

For the booking period Aug.18-28, I had flown my assistant guide and four guest hunters to the lodge. The Cub, N3421P, which I have owned since 1973, was performing perfectly. Compression was good on all four cylinders, oil consumption was low, and it was turning right at twenty-seven hundred rpm at full power. I've always babied my engines with oil changes every twenty-five hours, preheating if outside temperatures were below plus twenty degrees Fahrenheit, doing adequate warm ups prior to taking off and doing thorough annual inspections. This engine was no exception.

We had plenty of caribou in the valley near the lodge and an elderly Eskimo lady friend of mine, Beulah, had asked if I could bring her a cow caribou, including leggings and body skin. Her husband had passed away and she had no one to hunt for her. I told her that I would be happy to do so and should be able to provide a caribou soon, given the number of animals that were around my area.

The first day after getting everyone to the lodge, I did not put my assistant guide on the contract. A guide or assistant cannot hunt while contracted to guide others. That is a good law. As I was on the contract, I planned to have my assistant shoot a cow for Beulah. Since he was a resident of GMU 23 he could legally take fifteen caribou per day, every day of the year. Once he had a caribou for Beulah I could add him to the contract, and he could serve as my Assistant Guide the following day. Conditions were right and Beulah's caribou was secured and hung on the meat rack on the first day of the hunt.

As my assistant tended to Beulah's cow, I took two of the hunters further down the valley where one scored on a nice bull. Two of the guest hunters were using recurve bows and preferred to hunt by themselves.

Our efforts for the next few days did not result in another kill. Plenty of caribou were seen every day, but most were cows and calves. The bow hunters' self imposed weapons handicap had kept them from collecting their animals. The weather was warm, with little wind and the blow flies were out in force. I lightly salted the leggings and body skin of Beulah's cow and the cape of the bull and sprinkled ground black pepper liberally over all of the meat, to protect it from flies.

On the fourth day of the ten day booking we enjoyed grilled caribou steaks and a baked potato. I told everyone that I planned to take the meat to town in the morning as I needed to buy some more groceries. One of the bow hunters was consuming a full loaf of bread each day. It's hard to plan adequately for so voracious a consumer of groceries as that guy turned out to be.

Normally I am an early riser, but on the morning of day five I was awakened at about four o'clock a.m. by a nightmare. In my dream I was flying and ran out of gas. I awoke in a sweat. Bad dreams are not common to me, so I pay attention to the few that do come my way. I could not fall back to sleep.

When I got to the Cub with the meat I went through an extra thorough scrutinizing preflight, checking the fuel, gear and controls. Everything seemed fine. When I started the engine, it did not sound quite right, so I pulled the mixture to shut it down. I opened the cowling and checked everything again. All cylinders were warm, the plug wires were all snug, nothing was visibly amiss. Why was I so nervous? My nightmare had me twitchy.

On the second start, the engine sounded right, so I let it idle for several minutes to warm up adequately, then I departed. I

The first bull of the season.

still had an uneasy feeling, so I climbed as high as the cloud conditions would permit, to sixty-five hundred feet above ground level. The engine purred along. At five miles north of the Kotzebue airport, I reduced power to descend and the motor began to sound odd, then I heard a strange noise, I reduced power even more and about a mile and a half from the field, the rpms dropped to below eighteen hundred. I reduced power a bit more and landed easily on Runway one seven. I had enough extra altitude that I had to slip the Cub a bit to land and roll out adjacent to my tie down spot.

I pushed the Cub into its spot and tied it down. When I looked under the cowling, cylinder number two was not right. Later, a more thorough inspection revealed that it had swallowed a valve! I had a mechanic look at it. He said just replacing the cylinder and piston would not suffice, it needed a major overhaul.

Was I ever thankful for my nightmare, and that I had paid attention to it! That extra altitude as I crossed the north end of Kotzebue Sound made it possible for me to land on the runway, rather than some place short of it—like in the salt water of the Arctic Ocean!

The next morning I called Seattle and Texas for a replacement engine and learned that 0320 wide deck Lycoming engines were not lying about, ready to be shipped. None were immediately available.

Then I called John Alsworth in Anchorage.

He said, "Jake, remember that Lycoming one-fifty engine you gave me in 1976? I had given him the first engine that had failed me that year.

I replied, "Sure, John, but you don't still have that old thing sitting around do you?"

"No, but I have a high time engine belonging to my brother Glenn. It's kinda tired, but if you don't overload, it will get you through the season, and I'll ship it up to you this afternoon. You can take it off in Fairbanks when you're season is over and bring it back in your truck. It's pay back time!" he said.

Such a deal, such a friend.

That afternoon, my nephew, Ken Ubben, took me to the lodge in his Piper Super Cruiser (PA-12), to give the hunters the news and groceries. I told the men that I hoped to return in two to three days. We got to Kotzebue in time to meet the freighter that same afternoon. The mechanic and I began to remove the failed engine and we would be ready to begin hanging the replacement in the morning.

Weather turned sour with wind, rain and fog, but we had the use of a hanger—which was wonderful. In two days I had the chance to test fly the Cub and all seemed good.

That loaner engine got me through the season and back to Fairbanks where I pulled it off and returned it and the broken one to John. He over-hauled my defective engine and I rehung it the following summer of 2000.

Friendship like that of the Alsworth's is rare, and valuable beyond estimation.

911

On Sunday, September 9, 2001 I was at the lodge on Trail Creek—one hundred and eighteen miles due north of Kotzebue, Alaska, and approximately one hundred fifty-five miles above the Arctic Circle. Four guest hunters accompanied my sister, Pat, and me. I planned to fly a hunting guest back to Kotzebue that day. As had been my practice, I loaded the Cub just before departing for town to catch his scheduled morning departure the next day on the Alaska Airlines jet from Kotzebue. I listened to the local broadcast radio, KOTZ in Kotzebue, which reported generally light easterly winds throughout the Northwest Arctic. The forecast was for good weather and light winds.

My guest, a plumber named Bob whom I call Plumb Bob, had taken several caribou and a bull moose in the past twelve days with us. A slight breeze was blowing up the valley, permitting the easier down stream take off. Since this route has no brush or other obstructions, a bit heavier load could be easily and safely accommodated. With so much meat hanging on the rack, all of which I eventually would have to get to town, I drained five gallons of gas from the airplane to enable me to load an extra thirty pounds of meat. We departed heavy, but well within the safe and comfortable performance envelope of the Super Cub. At first, all went well, but when we departed the DeLong Mountains and started through the Noatak Flats, my GPS indicated we were making only about fifty miles per hour ground speed, though the airspeed was pegged at the usual ninety-five miles per hour. I climbed to thirty-five hundred feet, but at that altitude, the turbulence was uncomfortable, and our ground speed was even slower. It seemed the best ground speed could be found at about three hundred to five hundred feet above the surface. But as we neared Kotzebue we were showing only thirty to thirty-five miles per hour gain, in spite of a constant ninety-five mph air speed. In some places, our progress was even slower.

My radio was tuned into the Kotzebue Flight Service Station and I listened as other aircraft were advised of southeasterly winds at forty-eight gusting to fifty-six miles per hour. As we were by then about eighteen miles from town, with no safe river gravel bars to use due to the high water conditions, I scrutinized my gas gauges, which are small cork floats in glass tubes in the wing root on each side of the cockpit. When I raised a wing, I could see the top of the cork float up on that side, otherwise, when both wings were level, both sides appeared to be empty, with no sign of a float. I looked at my mini logbook which I keep handy with my sectional charts, and quickly calculated the time since I had last filled the tanks, deducted the five gallons I had drained out, and was confident that we could make it safely to the air strip, but not with a lot of fuel to spare. How I wished I had not drained out that five gallons of extra fuel!

If I could not get a "straight in" clearance to runway seventeen, I would consider declaring an emergency to avoid any delays, as even one time "around the patch" might be too much delay for our fuel supply. But by the time we were within the control zone, there were no other aircraft flying near the airfield.

Most people were smart enough to not be flying that afternoon, it appeared.

About three miles out, as we crossed the water of Kotzebue Sound, which is a part of the Arctic Ocean, I declared my intention to land "straight in" for runway 17. My request was approved, along with an update on the wind direction and speed, which were about the same as the last report I heard from the flight service station.

Plumb Bob, noticing my frequent glances at the fuel gauges, asked if I "was right sure I could get across the water without the engine quitting"?

"Yes, we have more than enough gas, trust me, Bob," I assured him.

"What if we don't?" he asked. I told him, then he should be ready to swim, as a landing in the mud flats we had been flying over for the past several miles would surely cause us to flip upside down, and only that mud and the ocean separated us from the field, so an intentional landing short of the field was simply out of the question.

Bob had flown with me many times and knew how to open the clam shell door of the Cub. But I suggested that he not practice that procedure at the moment.

Knowing I had a bit more fuel in the left tank than in the right one, I left the selector on the right tank until we were on short final approach to the dirt runway 17, at which time I switched to the left tank, as I knew that I would need to use some power to keep the aircraft from weather cocking in the strong, gusty cross wind conditions we was facing.

The wind was still coming from 250 degrees and blowing at forty-eight gusting to fifty-six mph. It was a gnarly, "white-knuckle," situation.

As we neared the threshold I allowed the plane to drift toward the right side of the runway, then I turned slightly left to diminish as much of the cross wind component as possible, rather than going straight down the gravel strip and taking the wind at a full eighty degrees across my route of flight. I lowered the left wing into the wind.

My Cub flies at about twenty-eight miles per hour, so with a wind well in excess of that, one must fly the plane onto the surface and dump the flaps using ailerons full into the windy side and applying opposite brake to avoid a ground loop. With such a strong wind in that great performing Super Cub, I had on several previous occasions landed cross ways on the strip. I planned to do that again. I drifted down over the dirt runway and didn't allow the wheels to touch the ground until we were opposite my tie downs. Then we touched the gravel, made a single gentle bounce, followed by a full stop. I doubt we used much more than twenty feet,—if that. I pulled the flaps down again, pushed the stick full forward, and, heavy as we were, the wind blew us back, but I asked Bob to get out and help guide the plane into it's tie down spot. He needed to get out and grab hold of the handle just forward of the horizontal stabilizer to steer and push the tail.

Plumb Bob performed well and we were in place, with tie-down ropes secured in less than two minutes after touching down.

No fuel showed on either gauge, but later, when I gassed up, it took thirty-three gallons to top off the tanks, meaning I had three gallons left, or about twenty-two minutes of flying time, and most of the remaining fuel was in the left wing tank. But that's way too thin for my comfort. I'd have much preferred to have carried thirty pounds less meat and the extra five gallons of fuel, if only I had known the wind was going to be so strong and from an adverse direction for so much of the one hundred and eighteen mile trip.

Oh well, hindsight is better than twenty-twenty, and anyway, we made it without mishap.

Plumb Bob insisted that I take his satellite telephone back up to the lodge, then return it to him when I got to Kodiak. I reluctantly agreed to do so. Plumb Bob was able to get a seat on the departing jet shortly after we arrived, so, with no reason or need to spend a night in town, I fueled up, loaded the Cub with fresh supplies and took full advantage of the strong tail wind back to the lodge.

I made record time returning to the lodge, arriving in fifty minutes instead of the usual ninety minute run. Though still very windy at five to six thousand feet, it was not so turbulent aloft and the wind in the valley of the lodge was only blowing about fifteen to twenty miles per hour, and it was only slightly cross wind to my main, eleven hundred foot runway.

The following day was very nice, so we hiked up the valley where my cousin Steve took a dandy bull caribou about four miles north of the lodge. Just before dark my sister, Pat, spotted a medium sized, blond grizzly across the creek, feeding on berries. We hustled over, but after climbing the cut bank, we decided the distance was too great to shoot, and darkness too imminent, to try to take the bear. We hoped that maybe we could locate it in the morning. The next day I was scheduled to take another hunter to Kotzebue, while my cousin, Steve Nason, recently out of the U.S. Marines, had two days left to hunt.

With the harrowing trip to town on Sunday, September 9 still fresh on my mind, on the morning of September 11, I used Bob's satellite phone to call the Kotzebue FAA Flight Service Station for current conditions.

The call was automatically transferred to the Fairbanks facility, from which a very agitated fellow told me that the United States was under heavy and serious military attack.

Several airliners had been hijacked. Pennsylvania, New York, Washington, D.C. and the Pentagon had been bombed, all civilian flights were grounded, and wartime conditions were at hand, he told me. He repeated that no civilian flights were to be made under any circumstances.

I told him to close my flight plan, as I was due to arrive in Kotzebue not later than six o'clock that evening. I also told him that I had a satellite telephone and I would call back. I was sure glad that Plumb Bob had convinced me to keep his phone.

I had made the call from the main room of the lodge and when I turned the phone off, my friend from Florida, Tom Minter, said something to the effect that from the look on my face, he knew something was badly wrong, and this was not one of my frequent pranks.

Carefully, I explained to everyone what I had heard and we went to the AM broadcast radio receiver in the

Steve Nason and his caribou taken on 9/10/01

lodge. Radio reception in the valley had deteriorated over what it had been twenty-five years earlier, but by meticulous tuning and sticking close to the set, we could faintly detect some of the news broadcast.

About two hours later, I again dialed the Kotzebue FAA Flight Service Station on the satellite phone and this time got a local "old hand" whose demeanor was calm, with more accurate facts. I reminded him that I had closed my flight plan, had a satellite phone, and that we were all fine.

Needless to say, we all stuck close to the radio, aghast at the news, wondering how far this terrorist onslaught would go. The name Bin Laden was mentioned several times.

I called home to Kodiak and told my wife, Teresa, to not take the children to school until I told her to do so. She replied that the local radio was reporting that the school district was advising all to attend school as usual. I told her to not let our kids go, and to not let anyone she didn't know—especially if they were wearing a turban—in the house, (I wanted to lighten her concerns, of course, so I emphasized turban). But no matter what she heard or what anybody else told her, our kids were to stay at home.

Cousin Steve Nason with the Bin Laden Bear, the lodge is visible just over Steve's left shoulder.

About mid-afternoon, my sister, Pat, spotted a large bear coming up the valley on the East side. I did not see it, but Pat knows her game, so Steve, Tom Minter and I went after it, leaving my Kodiak commercial fishing partner and best buddy, Tom Dooley and Pat at the lodge.

Another grizzly visited the meat pole in front of the lodge while we were in pursuit of the first one, so Pat put up the signal flag for us, but we did not see the flag until we had the first bear in range. Since this was definitely a big boar, I told Steve to take it, and he made a perfect "center punch" chest shot on the beast, which dropped to the tundra, stone dead. It squared over eight feet. It was indeed a very large inland grizzly. We called it the "Bin Laden Bear."

My cousin, Steve Nason, had been an exceptional marksman since his preteen years. I had trained him to shoot with a .22 rifle using iron sights. We often practiced shooting old tin cans thrown in the air. He had polished his skills to a fine edge and had recently completed a four year stint in the U.S. Marines as a sniper. He expressed his keen interest in having a chance to arrange a meeting between God and Bin Laden.

We toasted his bear and Steve's sentiments with the last of our whiskey.

That evening after supper and just before dark, with everyone's' ears and attention still affixed to the radio, Dooley heard a noise and hollered to me, "Partner, they's a helicopter coming up the valley, and it's got rockets on it!"

When Tom hollered, I was outside puttering around and heard the lub, lub, lub throbbing of the chopper blades. I grabbed my pistol, cranked one of our Honda three wheeler all terrane vehicles, turned the headlight on, and yelled "Everybody grab your rifles and ammunition and get away from the buildings!"

In what seemed like no time, a black helicopter was hovering within seventy meters of the lodge. I drove the Honda to the runway. The chopper turned and swiftly headed for the far end of our landing strip.

The helicopter was black and had no identifying insignia. It touched down just off the far end of our main runway, which is eleven hundred feet in length, putting the chopper about sixteen hundred feet from the lodge and well within rifle range, especially for Steve. I got off the Honda at about mid strip, leaving the engine running and the headlight on. One man in camouflage got out of the chopper and approached me.

"What's your name?" I hollered.

He replied, "Olanna, Sir!"

"You from Shishmaref?" I shouted.

"No, but my Dad is, Sir," he replied.

"Are you National Guard?" I asked.

"Yes, Sir."

"Then have the pilot turn the machine off and have all the crew come up for a coffee and a piece of hot blue berry pie," I told him.

"My pilot didn't like what he saw happening here and won't approach. We just wanted to be sure you were okay, then we have to get back to Nome. By the way, do you need anything? " the soldier replied.

"Olanna, if you'd been wearing a turban, my cousin would have seen to it that you wouldn't have a head just now. Why aren't there any markings on that chopper and why don't you use a bull horn in situations like this?" I asked.

"And, oh yeah, we're out of booze, can you supply any?"

He replied that he would relay the information regarding identifying insignia and a bull horn. He added that we should just sit tight and unfortunately, they had no booze for us. With that, he boarded the helicopter and it departed directly down valley.

It's noteworthy that the chopper did not fly past the lodge again before exiting the valley.

But I got video footage of their departure.

Several days later, when I finally got to Kotzebue, I heard from a relative of the chopper pilot that the leaders at the National Guard Headquarters in Nome felt like they needed to "just do something," so they decided to check on us, as they agreed that "it is so pretty at Jacobson's camp." Nome is a long way from our lodge at Trail Creek ... but it surely is pretty at our place.

Weeks later, I learned that the Kotzebue Civil Air Patrol commander had been chewed out for not sending a CAP plane up to check on us, as my Emergency Locator Transmitter was sending signals, or so the official was said to have reported.

I contacted the CAP to tell them the story of my ELT going off was not true, and the chopper people never mentioned anything about an ELT signal when they were at the lodge.

Still later, CAP indicated that the National Guard flight was undertaken because the CAP did not have a plane available to check on me, as I was overdue on my (twice closed) flight plan.

That's government for you. It seemed obvious to me that the National Guard had been chewed out for the unnecessary trip all the way to Trail Creek—well over three hundred miles, and they were trying to cover their actions ... or assets ... or something.

I contacted the "old hand" from the Kotzebue Flight Service Station who verified that indeed, I had closed my flight plan. He had a recording of our telephone conversation during which I closed my plan for the second time that same morning. I got an official letter from FAA about the incident verifying closure of my flight plan, and I wrote a letter to the National Guard demanding to know why the chopper had no easily readable identifying marks on it and no megaphone for situations like we had experienced. Those two issues were specially important on a day like September 11, 2001.

Both the National Guard and the Civil Air Patrol were getting some flack from higher ups. The Guard was trying to justify the chopper flight from Nome to Trail Creek, so they came up with the ELT story. Civil Air Patrol headquarters tried to help the Guard cover-up by reporting me overdue on a flight plan. But, the FAA recording of me closing my flight plan placed the responsibility—or blame, if you will—where it belonged. Which was on the National Guard.

I never got an answer to my letter to the Alaska National Guard.

Sluggin' My Way To Fairbanks

Only four hundred and forty miles separate Kotzebue, Alaska from Fairbanks—that's if you're able to fly a direct course between the two hub communities. A Global Positioning System (GPS) helps minimize the travel distance and flying time.

The direct route, well—any route, actually—passes over some of the wildest, most remote territory in the nation, but luckily, there are several villages with airports scattered along the way. And there are a few other areas suitable for an unscheduled landing.

Assuming a straight course with no influence from wind, a Piper Super Cub, can make that trip in a bit under five hours, if no landing is required. Over the past forty years I have flown that route more than one hundred times. My fastest trip was from Kotzebue to Fairbanks in four hours fifteen minutes, flying a direct course at an altitude of fifty-five hundred feet with a tailwind. My slowest trip, also from West to East took nearly nine hours, but in addition to significant head wind, on that trip I also had to divert around some foul weather.

Given the possibility for adverse conditions, I always top off the eighteen gallon main tank in each wing and fill the thirty-two gallon belly tank, no matter which way I am going. The total of sixty-eight gallons is practically all usable. Well … maybe a gallon or so might not transfer out of the belly into the left wing tank. I calculate my flying time by figuring on burning about eight gallons of hundred octane aviation fuel per hour, but actually my engine consumes about seven and a half gallons per hour. The higher I'm able to fly, the more I can lean the fuel mixture, burning even less fuel and resulting in more than nine hours of flying time … but I don't count on that.

When I was ready to make the trip back to Fairbanks in 2009 the weather was forecast as good VFR (Visual Flight Rules) conditions for the route on Thursday and Friday. It was late September and each day lost about eight minutes of daylight. So, we were losing nearly an hour per week in this area adjacent to the Arctic Circle, but we still were getting over eleven hours of daylight. I had a miserable head cold when I woke up on Thursday, so I postponed the flight until Friday. A large occluded front was due to hit Fairbanks on Saturday and worsening weather with IFR (Instrument Flight Rules) conditions in snow and icing were predicted to last for two or three days, but it looked like a good bet to hold off until Friday, in view of my battle with the viral condition. I just didn't feel at all good and planned to spend most of the day in bed, which I did.

Friday morning, September 25, I felt better. The sun rose about 10:30am. My Super Cub was fueled, loaded and ready to go. I stopped by the Flight Service Station (FSS) for an updated en route forecast and current conditions from nearby reporting stations. Many of the villages had automated weather stations which reported each hour, which is a huge improvement over the situation of a few years ago when only the major hubs reported weather.

The fellows in the FSS told me it should be a good VFR trip. Then one of them said "Jake, things look perfect, it should be an easy trip." I replied that I always dreaded hearing the word "perfect" as it usually resulted in me having to slug my way through the "perfect" area. Maybe I'm semi-superstitious, but I've seen it happen that way more often than not.

Departure from Kotzebue at eleven o'clock that morning was easy with a North wind blowing about ten knots, I took off on the paved runway zero niner. As always, the Cub was loaded to the max—volume wise—but my load, which included a warm down sleeping bag, tent, firearm, ax, shovel, stove with fuel and emergency food, as well as a sandwich, an apple, some cookies, a quart of water and thermos of coffee, was not heavy. Oh, I also had a quart of pickled beluga muktuk, a last minute gift from my daughter, Sandy, for snacking on as I traveled.

The two thousand foot overcast at Kotzebue lifted as I flew east, so I took the Cub higher and picked up a bit of tailwind—which is better than money in the bank. By the time I reached the Purcell Mountains, about one fourth the distance, I was cruising at 5,500 feet, had the mixture leaned back and was indicating ninety-five miles per hour air speed, but the GPS showed one hundred to one hundred five miles per hour ground speed, due to the tailwind component of the winds aloft. I kept a heading of zero-eight-eight degrees—nearly dead East. The trip, so far, had been as perfect as the forecasters predicted.

My direct route of flight took me just south of the village of Hughs where the GPS indicated I was traveling at only 85 mph ground speed with the airspeed still pegged at ninety-five. A little headwind was slowing me down, but I was a bit over halfway to my destination.

Still on the direct route to Fairbanks, I crossed the Yukon River and was just south of Minto village which is about fifty miles West of Fairbanks. I could hear VHF radio traffic at Fairbanks International Airport which was indicating good VFR conditions, but I saw a dense snow squall just in front of me. Those formerly friendly skies were starting to look downright sullen up ahead.

Many times I have gone "VFR on top" if my intended destination was reporting broken or better conditions that would allow an easy descent, but this time I wasn't sure I could get back down through the cloud cover if I went on top, so I reduced my altitude to go under or through the snow squall ahead. The outside air temperature was plus twenty degrees. I anticipated dropping under the cloud bank, then coming out the other side, while still in the Minto Flats area. I figured I would then climb back to thirty-five hundred feet or so, to get over the hills between me and Chena Marina, where I planned to tie down the Cub for the winter.

As I entered the snowy conditions, I turned on my navigation lights and rotating beacon. I wanted to avoid any other aircraft that might be in that snowy soup. I had to keep getting lower and lower, until I was just above the tree tops. But I had manageable visibility of over one mile and believed I could just turn back to Minto if necessary.

Then I went through a patch of freezing rain. A glance at my outside air thermometer indicated plus thirty-four degrees.

After just a few seconds there was ice on the wings and the windshield. I decided to follow a small winding stream down current, catch the Tanana River, fly over Nenana and then go on to Fairbanks. I turned my cabin heat on full and placed the flexible heater hose near the windshield. Slowly the ice began to clear in the center of my windshield. Gradually, reluctantly, the diameter of the melted area increased, giving me a wider view.

Then my airspeed indicator dropped to zero. My Pitot/Static tube had frozen closed, denying the instrument the airflow it required to register my speed. I had no way to de-ice that system.

And I began feeling the buffeting of moderate turbulence.

After ten minutes or so I found the Tanana River, banked left and flew upstream toward Nenana. I kept expecting to break out of the soup into good VFR conditions, which would hopefully be warm enough to rid the plane of the increasing ice load it was steadily accumulating.

My GPS was working, but I stayed just over the river as visibility was dropping to an uncomfortable level and I kept having to add power to maintain the altitude I needed. I knew the need for more power meant ice was building up on the exterior and the increasing weight on the plane could necessitate a forced landing on a river bar. I could see a coating of clear ice on the leading edge of my wings and it seemed to be thickening.

The bars on the Chena River are composed of soft sand and silt and were littered with piles of logs and brush residue from recent high water. The jumble of drift wood on the river bars and banks reminded me of scenes of the aftermath of a tornado. And I saw no bars that looked like they were amenable to a safe landing—let alone a take-off, when conditions got better. So, I kept grinding along over that forever muddy river.

Visibility varied as I flew along through one little squall to the next. I turned my landing and taxi lights on. The outside air temperature remained between thirty and thirty-five degrees.

And I whispered a prayer that I was in need of help, as my situation was becoming more and more uncomfortable.

After what seemed like much too long, my GPS showed Nenana only nine miles ahead, but I stayed just over the river and did not turn to go directly to the town—in case I needed to make an emergency landing. I kept adding small increments of throttle to maintain altitude. Several times I pulled carburetor heat, but there was no indication of carburetor icing.

I could not leave the engine at full throttle without risking damage to the power plant, so after gaining a bit of altitude and trimming the plane for cruise at seventy-two miles per hour, I would reduce the throttle until I had to add more power to maintain altitude.

Then I saw the strobe atop the bridge over the Tanana River. I had to give the Cub full throttle to get above the bridge, but due to the increasing load of ice, I lost some altitude as I flew down the Parks Highway as it passed through the town of Nenana. Automated street lights were lit on either side of me at about eye level. I knew I could land on the highway, but it was paved with a layer of snow and ice atop the tarmac. The wind was gusty and I figured I should try to keep airborne until I reached the old military runway or a dirt road nearby. Breaking would be minimal on that icy highway. I did not like the prospect of landing on the paved highway, only to have the wind slide the plane off the icy surface into a drainage ditch on either side of the road.

About a mile down the paved highway I turned left, found a narrow dirt road with a sufficiently straight stretch leading to the runway. When I pulled the throttle back to descend, the now heavy Cub dropped noticeably faster than normal. Near the surface I feathered out and gently set the plane down on the road, almost directly into the gusty wind. I touched down in the soft field manner—main wheels and tail wheel contacting the road simultaneously with only a minimal bump. But I heard ice slide off the wings and crackle as it hit the ground. The road had some medium sized potholes in it and each one I taxied through caused more ice to fall off the wings and other surfaces.

But, I was happy to be there. It was only a short taxi to the paved runway. A slight berm at the junction of the road and runway was enough to bring more ice off the Cub.

On the ramp off to one side of the runway sat several aircraft, so I taxied in between two tail draggers and pulled the mixture to shut down the engine. Before I began to search for tie down rings, I gave Thanks for my safe arrival.

It was clear to me that I would not be flying any further that day, so I called Fairbanks Flight Service Station on my cell phone to give them my location and tell them to close my flight plan. If this is not done, within a half hour of a plane being overdue, FSS will begin to call, then set the wheels in motion for a search. I did not want to have anyone flying out in that storm looking for me.

The last forty minutes or so of that flight was the most tense time that I could recall in my forty-two years of piloting small aircraft in Alaska. I recalled that the Flight Service Station guys in Kotzebue assured me that it was a "perfect" day for the trip. That's a jinx, for sure!

The tie down rings were large screw eyes set down in holes in the pavement to make the top of the rings flush with the surface. As a sheet of ice covered the surface, it took some searching to find the rings, then, with a screwdriver, I chipped out ice enough to permit me to pass my ropes through the rings. The wind was gusty, making outside work uncomfortable. Some of the gusts caused my little airplane to slide slightly on the ice rink upon which it sat, until I could stop its motion with the ropes.

Mixed rain and snow were falling, as two men in a small pick-up drove over to me and stopped.

"Hey, we just saw you fly right over the street lights in Nenana! We're sure glad to see you here," one said.

"Yep, I'm glad to see me here, too," was my reply.

"What are you going to do now?," the fellow named Don Zink asked.

"After tying down the plane, I'm going to unload some of my gear and hike to town, maybe get a room for the night or however long this ice storm lasts," I told him.

"Do you like to chop wood?," Don asked.

"I can't think of a more appealing activity in this sort of situation," I told him.

"Well, we're here to chop wood for the manager of the Christian radio station. If you'd like to help, we can put you up for the night at the church and share some supper with you," he offered.

"That sounds like a heck of a deal, but I have a tent and can get by, or find a room in town, if it would be an inconvenience to you," I assured him.

"Oh, you better come with us, besides we'd like to hear where you came from, how the trip was, and so forth," he assured me.

And so it was that I enjoyed supper with these men and the radio station manager's family and did not need to set up my tent or find a hotel room. We had an enjoyable evening swapping stories after dinner.

Saturday morning looked about like the previous evening with low visibility in mixed rain and wet snow. After breakfast we drove out to check the airplane, which by then had accumulated a heavy new coating of ice. Wet sticky snow was falling, so I used a broom to sweep off what I could and decided to leave what didn't come off easily to minimize wear and tear on the fabric of the wings. There's no sense fighting ice off fabric surfaces if you don't need to fly, as temperature swings will often cause the ice to melt away of its own accord.

We drove down the road a few miles to the fire wood site where we split some, but mostly just tossed already split wood into a loader and stacked it. It was all nice birch, so much better than the Sitka spruce we use at Kodiak. The work was not hard and I kept reminding myself how pleasant this all was, compared to being on one of those nasty sand bars in a tent for the night and figuring out how I'd get the plane airborne when the weather improved.

Weather conditions remained about the same throughout the day, with an occasional "sucker hole" briefly appearing. I was never tempted to fly that day.

On Sunday morning the sky cover was "broken" but very amenable to VFR flight, so the men dropped me off at the plane, then drove on to attend a church service in Fairbanks. I set about getting ready to depart. The temperature was plus twenty-six degrees Fahrenheit, so pre-heating the engine was not necessary.

Not all the ice and snow must be removed, but it must be "polished" to allow a smooth flow of air over the wings. The fuselage and horizontal stabilizer, rudder and all parts should be in similar condition.

The top of all wings (or airfoils) is somewhat curved, while the lower side is flat. Thus, when in flight, the longer distance for air to travel over the top of the wing produces a negative upward force which results in "lift." If the wings are not smooth, the air flow will not be uniform which can result in "burbles" which decrease or destroy lift. If ice forms during flight, the motion through the air is usually enough to cause the added ice to adhere smoothly, but too much additional weight can quickly become a dangerous problem. In my ten thousand-plus hours of bush flight experiences in Alaska, most of the ice that formed in flight usually was gone by the time I landed. But it did not happen that way on this trip.

It took over three hours to get the plane de-iced and ready for the short hop to Fairbanks, a mere thirty-five miles away, but I am sure I could not have made it without the stop in Nenana. I used my cell phone to call FSS in Fairbanks and filed a flight plan. I got the engine started and waited until my cylinder head temperature was over one hundred degrees and the oil temperature was showing over eighty degrees.

During my taxi, I noticed the tires slipping in places on the pavement—the ice was still covering everything, except my airplane. Take-off was routine and the short flight to Fairbanks was unremarkable. The dirt strip at Chena Marina had been drug to clear the snow and I landed without a problem. Dirt strips are much more forgiving than paved surfaces.

It was Sunday afternoon, so after getting tied down I quickly drained the oil from the engine and put in the pickling oil that my mechanic friend, Jimmy Anderson, had placed next to the furnace in the hangar. A twenty minute run-up with the sticky preservative lubricant in the crankcase, followed by placement of the dryer plugs in the top spark plug holes, removal of the battery, ELT, radios, seat, tools and emergency equipment and I was just about ready to kiss the Cub good night until the next summer.

Still feeling lucky, I needed to hit the road early the next morning to get to Anchorage and then down to Homer to catch the state ferry to Kodiak. I chased around the grocery stores looking for a big turkey. Finally I found one to drop by the radio station manager's house in Nenana as partial thanks for the meals I had enjoyed at his home. By nine o'clock that evening I had things pretty well taken care of, so I stopped at a Wendy's for a double burger and headed for the one room log cabin I used when in Fairbanks.

The next morning the Maule flown by Buck Maxson, with my nephew, Ken Ubben aboard, landed at Chena Marina. They had been a few miles behind me when they encountered the freezing rain and had to land at Tanana, a bit over one hundred miles west of where I landed. Whether it's a hundred miles or a half mile, when it's time to quit flying, it's time to quit—before you absolutely have to do so.

The residue of the ice storm was more evident Monday than the day before. Weather had turned down right miserable again. Apparently the occluded front had stalled in its northerly journey and bounced back. The roads were hazardous in ice and visibility was poor in mixed rain and snow. I was happy to have gotten in the day before and to be only driving a truck through the nasty stuff now, instead of flying a small airplane.

The fifty or so miles to Nenana by road were slow going with several cars off into the snow and abandoned on either side. Ahead of me I saw one small compact car slip, then start to spin, before catching a deep snow berm and going off the road. I stopped to offer assistance. The young lady driving was shaken up, but not injured, and she gratefully accepted my offer for a ride the eighteen miles to Nenana where she could arrange for a tow truck to pull her vehicle back onto the highway. She said she had good insurance and did not want me to try to pull her out with my truck. I had a fifty foot length of heavy crab line for such purposes, but it was too short for that job. Considering the curve her car was on, the icy road surface, and the steepness of the bank the car had slipped over, I agreed with her decision to have a professional do it.

After getting her squared away with a local tow truck operator I dropped the turkey by the radio station manager's house. When I knocked, his five year old daughter opened the door and asked if I was back with my airplane.

"No, my airplane is in Fairbanks and all bundled up for the winter. But do you like turkey?" I questioned.

"Well yes, we love turkey," she told me.

When I gave her the frozen bird she asked where I had found it.

"Oh, I found it up the road a ways, but I don't have room for it, so I thought you and your family could put it to good use," I explained.

The manager's wife came to the door and told me that I didn't have to do that.

"Yes, Missus, I did have to do it ... for my own satisfaction and thank you for the kind hospitality you offered to a complete stranger," I said.